# LEGAL ASPECTS OF MENTAL RETARDATION

# LEGAL ASPECTS OF MENTAL RETARDATION

## A SEARCH FOR RELIABILITY

*By*

ROBERT HENLEY WOODY, Ph.D.

*Professor of Education and Psychology*
*The Ohio University*
*Athens, Ohio*
*and*
*Consulting Psychologist in Private Practice*

CHARLES C THOMAS · PUBLISHER
*Springfield · Illinois · U.S.A.*

*Published and Distributed Throughout the World by*
CHARLES C THOMAS • PUBLISHER
Bannerstone House
301-327 East Lawrence Avenue, Springfield, Illinois, U.S.A.


ISBN 0-398-03243-2
Library of Congress Catalog Card Number: 74-8305

*With THOMAS BOOKS careful attention is given to all details of manufacturing and design. It is the Publisher's desire to present books that are satisfactory as to their physical qualities and artistic possibilities and appropriate for their particular use. THOMAS BOOKS will be true to those laws of quality that assure a good name and good will.*

*Printed in the United States of America*
*A-2*

**Library of Congress Cataloging in Publication Data**

Woody, Robert Henley.
Legal aspects of mental retardation.

1. Mental health laws—United States. 2. Forensic psychiatry. I. Title. [DNLM: 1. Jurisprudence. 2. Mental retardation. W740 W912L 1974]
KF480.W66 344'.73'0323 74-8305
ISBN 0-398-03243-2

## DEDICATION

Once there were four brothers: Arthur, Joe, Charlie, and Bob—the latter was my father. These brothers, collectively, were not unusual for their time. They were from the rural south and were relatively uneducated. Three of them, however, were able to obtain steady employment, marry, have children and homes, obtain property and possessions, and have experiences that go along with everyday life, while one of them—Arthur—was never able to do so. He was mentally retarded. Within his small town in the south, he was accepted and allowed to move around through the community; he disturbed no one and people recognized that he was "not very bright." In fact, the local foundry even employed him for several years to work alongside his brothers and his father as a helper. But then his father and mother died, and his brothers, hoping to improve their lot in life, migrated north in search of employment that would let them bring in higher incomes and thus be "better providers" for their families. Arthur was forced to go along, but the more complex life styles, even in a fairly small midwestern city, created new problems: he could not go out alone for fear of being lost; he was unable to cope successfully with the hustle and bustle of traffic and people; and he was not readily accepted by the community—after all, he was a "stranger in a strange land." The family tried to continue to care for him, but he was uncomfortable with the environs, and they had their own responsibilities and aspirations to meet. Eventually, it became evident that the family could no longer care for him properly, and he was voluntarily (albeit reluctantly) placed in a state institution. As can best be determined, he received no "treatment" and remained consistently in a depersonalized custodial situation. The family did not know how to improve his conditions. I was but an adolescent then, and they, with their cultural background, assumed that the state institution would "do everything possible"; there was no money within the family to obtain special services. Arthur eventually died, allegedly from an "unexplained fall" within the state institution.

This book is dedicated to my father and his brothers, with the intention that this will symbolize a concern for the many other families that are faced with a similar problem: having a loved one in need of special services, but feeling powerless to arrange for effective interventions and/or placements. The contents of this book are especially designed to increase professionals' awareness of legal aspects of mental retardation in order that they may more effectively intervene on behalf of mentally retarded clients and their families.

# PREFACE

PUBLIC SERVICE is a demanding role, regardless of how it is manifested. By definition, this means that the service is extended to any citizen needing and/or requesting it, and this introduces a multitude of human factors with which the worker in public service must reckon. Most pronounced, no doubt, is dealing with individuals who are different than the majority of people; in other words, the deviant or exceptional.

Being deviant and/or exceptional often carries a positive connotation, such as the elite intellectual, or it may carry a very negative connotation, such as the criminal group. Somewhere in between these extremes are those persons who are in need of special help because of handicapping conditions. The person with a physical ailment typically receives sympathetic help, whereas the person with a socio-cultural ailment (such as those who might be on "welfare rolls") usually receives, at most, hostile tolerance rather than sympathy.

It is a different story for those persons with mental problems. This would include those who suffer a clinically diagnosed mental illness and those who have been identified (hopefully through a professional diagnosis) as mentally retarded (note that the term "mentally retarded" is used generically, and is encompassing of "mental defective," "mentally subnormal," and "mentally handicapped"). Both the mentally ill and the mentally retarded have received an increasing amount of public understanding over the past two decades. Accordingly, legislation and funding for special services and programs have resulted. There are, however, still many distinct societally-based systems that do not give just, effective service to persons with mental problems.

The American legal system is one such source, and this book is devoted to attempting to upgrade the situation via focusing attention on the legal aspects of mental retardation. This is not to say that the legal system has been blind to the needs of the mentally retarded (or the mentally ill): quite to the contrary. It does, however, seem fair to assert that *the mentally retarded have not received optimal consideration within our contemporary legal system* (and a retrospective look at legal accounts involving mentally retarded persons creates unquestionably an even more appalling picture).

After years of practical involvement as a professional psychologist and after an analysis of relevant legal publications, I believe that the neglect of the legal aspects of mental retardation is due to two reasons. First, there has been a lack of communication between professionals in the health and behavioral sciences and those in law. While this may be a naive or, at times, perhaps even a justifiable distrust of professionals from a discipline other than one's own, it may also be a reflection of the difficulty inherent to communicating about mental retardation. Mental retardation, as will be clarified in this book, is more than "being dumb." It is more than an intellectual deficit pure and simple. In addition to the intellectual limitations, it involves a myriad of psychological and social factors that tie into the need for special accommodations for behavioral adaptations. Second, and this is a "difficult pill to swallow" for many professionals, the mentally retarded person is not "an attractive client," and thus, consciously or unconsciously, the professional (regardless of discipline) is apt to by-pass the mentally retarded person in favor of a more interesting client. It is a truism that both lawyers and counselors/psychotherapists do not find the mentally retarded person to be as professionally stimulating as other types of clients. Thus the mentally retarded are neglected by practitioners; and without the attention of practitioners, bringing about change within a service system will be difficult. Restated, if legal, health, behavioral science, and educational personnel (to name but a few of the disciplinary sources) do not give pragmatic attention to the mentally retarded, there will be no press on those in authority over the system, such as the legislators and judiciary personnel relevant to the legal system, to bring about needed changes to properly accommodate mentally retarded clients.

This book is directed, in part, at stimulating lay and professional persons alike to work toward maximum benefits for the mentally retarded within our legal system. To achieve this goal, information about mental retardation is presented and legal aspects relevant to mental retardation are discussed. For the legal specialist, the information about mental retardation may be the most meaningful; for the mental retardation specialist, the information about the legal aspects may have the most value. For the layman, perhaps both areas of information will lead to increased knowledge.

While one goal is to stimulate responsible actions from laymen and professionals, perhaps the primary goal is to create an awareness of the need to make the legal system reliable in serving the mentally retarded (and it should go without saying that reliable service should be available to all, mentally retarded or otherwise). Therefore, attention is devoted throughout the book to the relevance of the concept of reliability to the given topic.

The format of the book attempts to develop a continuum: from the definition of the concept of reliability (Chapter One) and mental retardation (Chapter Two); through diagnostic practices (Chapter Three) and nosological/classification systems (Chapter Four); to the more legal issues of the mental retardation/criminality hypothesis (Chapter Five), the rights (Chapter Six) and liability (Chapter Seven) of the mentally retarded, the administrative and judicial procedures (Chapter Eight) and the expert testimony (Chapter Nine) available to the mentally retarded; and to the culminating frame of reference for responsible actions (Chapter Ten).

The contents of this book should make it a suitable reference source for practitioners and a supplementary text for college and university courses (and in-service training programs) for such areas as law, law enforcement, medicine (particularly psychiatry), health sciences (especially health education and administration), psychology (including the school, counseling, and clinical specialties), social work, rehabilitation and community services, guidance and counseling, religious education, and special education.

Working on this book has been personally rewarding. As mentioned in the *Dedication,* there were familial elements that spurred my interest. Further, since my first position as a psychologist required focusing on psychological assessments and counseling for mentally retarded persons and their families, I found a host of scenes, some going back many years, being replayed in my mind as I culled published accounts. Thus I believe that I grew personally and professionally through this endeavor and I hope that the reader can experience the same.

Special appreciation is expressed to my wife, Jane Divita Woody, Ph.D., M.S.W.; in addition to contributing immeasurable domestic conditions that facilitated work on the book, she used her professional expertise to edit the manuscript. Also Professor Michael Jon Kindred, J.D. (Ohio State University College of Law) stimulated me to pursue study in the area of legal aspects of mental retardation and offered helpful criticisms of the first draft. Ms. Pamela Borton deserves commendation for dutifully (and cheerfully) typing and retyping the manuscript. Finally, I must thank my children, Bobby and Jenny, for their cooperation: with all the wisdom of five and six year old children, they generously relinquished (temporarily) their father-playmate because "Daddy's got to work on a book."

R.H.W.

# CONTENTS

# LEGAL ASPECTS OF MENTAL RETARDATION

## CHAPTER ONE

# RELIABILITY AND LEGAL PROCESSES FOR THE MENTALLY RETARDED

PROVIDING SERVICES to deviant or exceptional persons within our society is no easy task. The reasons for this are many. The mere status of being "deviant" or "exceptional" denotes variance from the majority and from the accepted norms. Because of these differences, the "normals" formulate a unique set of attitudes toward these "exceptional" persons. Further, each deviant or exceptional person is idiosyncratic. That is, persons cannot justly be lumped together into nondistinguishing categories; they must be dealt with as individuals with a composite of psychological-social-physiological characteristics that is never exactly the same as that maintained by others in a similar category.

Mental retardation, as a concept, would be simple enough if it could be viewed and treated solely as an intellectual deficit. Unfortunately, as will emerge in the subsequent pages, it is more than that: true, there is typically a significant impairment in one or more intellectual areas, but there is also a complex set of behavioral adaptations, some of which may be directly related to mental retardation *per se,* while some may be totally unrelated yet be erroneously considered to be manifestations of mental retardation.

Because of this complexity, it is not surprising that societal systems, since they were developed to handle the needs of the masses, frequently have trouble accommodating adequately the needs of the deviant or exceptional individual. Public education is a prime example of a societal system that has had to cope with this problem. Until the establishment of special education programs (which must still be viewed as being in their infancy, since they are prone to be directed primarily at the handicapped exceptional person to the neglect of the gifted exceptional person), public schools commonly treated all children relatively the same: Every child was expected to fit into a regular classroom, and if their idiosyncratic qualities, i.e. their exceptionality, led to ineffective learning or behavioral maladjustment in this context, they (and their parents) were responsible for either adapting to the school's expectations or making other arrangements (such as dropping out of school).

Much like the public educational system, the legal system has had difficulties in acknowledging and accommodating deviancy and exceptionality. This is probably particularly true because of the number of cases involving alleged and/or proven criminal acts. But it must be remembered that the legal system is designed for more than criminal acts, and criminal stereotyping cannot be allowed; i.e. exceptional persons must not be subjected to discrimination within the very system that is supposed to protect their rights as well as the rights of society. In many instances, unfortunately, illogical, unjust stereotyping has occurred with mentally retarded persons.

Mentally retarded persons, by virtue of their exceptionality, have long been the source of problematic consternation for the American legal system. Two of the most pronounced challenges placed before the legal authorities have been: (1) the proper consideration of the ramifications of "mental retardation" within the legal processes; and (2) the upholding of rights in spite of the fact that the mentally retarded person has been assigned by society to a special class of citizenry.

One of the major concomitants of these two challenges is the need for legal personnel to be *objectively informed* about mental retardation. It is only through such a stance that they can interpret and develop the law to accommodate mental retardation. While much of the responsibility rests directly on the shoulders of the legal profession (e.g. law schools should provide training in the behavioral sciences), the responsibility must be shared by those in the "helping professions," e.g. medical doctors, psychologists, social workers, counselors, educators, and other representatives from the clergy, health sciences, rehabilitation and social services, and law enforcement.

This book is devoted to exploring numerous aspects of the legal system that affect mentally retarded persons. In addition to providing information about "mental retardation" *per se,* the focus will be on the concept of *reliability.* Although a more thorough definition will be subsequently posited, suffice it to say that the concept of reliability in this context refers to factors that assure that consistency of legal processes will be provided to the mentally retarded. The concept of reliability is also directed at obtaining objectivity in dealing with human behavior and characteristics, whether it be with a mentally retarded person or anyone else.

## THE RELIABILITY CONCEPT

In any form of measurement, from the most off-the-cuff judgment or appraisal of something to the most statistically sophisticated measuring device or test, there are two primary concepts: the *validity* concept and the *reliability* concept. The validity concept, stated simply, is reflected in how *accurately* the appraisal procedure does, in fact, measure what it purports to measure. The reliability concept, likewise stated simply, is reflected in how *consistently* the appraisal procedure does, in fact, measure what it purports to measure; or as Kelly (1967) states: "In the simplest terms, the reliability of any measuring device refers to the precision with which it measures whatever it measures."

As might be anticipated, these two concepts become inextricably interwoven in measurement procedures. It is a truism of measurement that: *It is possible for an appraisal method to be reliable but be lacking in validity, but it is impossible for an appraisal method to be valid and be lacking in reliability.* In other words, for any valid measure to be made (be it an evaluating opinion about someone's behavior or a judgment about a set of circumstances), there must be reliability.

The definition of "reliability" can be simplistic; for example, Mitchell (undated) provides the following definition for reliability: "The extent to which a test is consistent in measuring whatever it does measure; dependability, stability, trustworthiness, relative freedom from errors of measurement. Reliability is usually expressed by some form of *reliability coefficient* or by the *standard error of measurement* derived from it." The simplicity of the definition, however, rapidly turns into complexity because of two sets of properties: mathematical and human qualities.

In brief, the mathematical properties intrinsic to measurement reliability deal with the variance produced by the measurement procedure, method, or test itself. In other words, if every intervening variable were held constant and a test was administered and then readministered at a later time, there would, in all probability, still be differences between the two obtained measurement values. Even with a single score, it might be expected that variance, though undetermined in the single measurement, might be inherent because of the mathematical properties of the evaluation procedure; and the same would be true with repeated measures:

> Then, it seems reasonable to ask what proportion of the observed or measured differences . . . is attributable to true or actual differences. . . . If this proportion is large, then the measurements reflect true differences; on the other hand, if the proportion is small, a large part of what has been observed is error. This proportion of the amount of variation in true scores to the total variation has been given the name *reliability*. Thus, in terms of tests, reliability is defined as the ratio of the true score variance to the variance in the scores as observed. (Helmstadter, 1964.)

Related to the standard error of measurement that occurs in appraisals, another major source of error is *chance circumstances*. Kleinmuntz (1967) discusses the variation that occurs because of random or chance error: "There are many sources of chance error that contribute to score variation from one measurement to the next. Such chance error, or error variance, can be due to poor test environment, fatigue, eye-strain, luck in selecting certain answers, ambiguously worded items, errors in scoring, and a host of other possible sources. Essentially any condition that is extraneous to the purpose of the test, and influences the test score in undetermined ways, contributes to error variance."

A parenthetical example was noted in a large state prison: a six-tiered quadrangle of cells formed a perimeter for an area which, on the open ground floor had a small cement block structure where all psychological tests were administered. As an inmate went to the psychologist for testing, he walked across the open area under the eyes of literally hundreds of other prisoners (and taunts about "going to see the headshrinker" were commonplace): There seems little doubt that these environmental factors influenced the results of the psychological testing!

Human qualities constitute the second set of properties that makes the concept of reliability complex. Any human who formulates a judgment has the potential, regardless of academic training and regardless of personal qualities, to be biased; and bias is part of subjectivity, and subjectivity automatically makes the reliability of the judgment vulnerable to achieving less than optimum status.

These processes are typically cast into the rubric of *clinical judgment.* It should be noted that the term "clinical" does not refer necessarily to professionals within the realm of "clinical medicine," but is generic enough to encompass any professional, such as attorneys and judges, who processes information for the formulation of expert opinions and/or decision-making. Thorne (1961), one of the foremost researchers in the area of clinical judgment, states:

> Most parsimoniously, *clinical judgment* properly refers simply to the correctness of the *problem-solving thinking of a special class of persons,* namely clinically trained persons with special levels of training, experience and competence. Judgments concerning clinical matters can be made by anyone. Such *lay opinions* have only the weight of the level of intelligence, education and experience of the person making them. It always remains to be demonstrated whether specialty training and experience make possible judgments of higher validity than lay opinions.

Note that this last sentence is one that is readily applicable to a long-term controversy in law; i.e. the question is whether expert opinion or lay opinion (the jury) should make the decision regarding guilt or innocence. Thorne (1961) further notes:

> Theoretically, at least, the qualifications of (a) being highly selected as to ability, (b) having the highest levels of training, and (c) possessing the highest levels of experience, make the clinician the most competent person to make *clinical* decisions according to the highest

> standards of time and place. So, the competent clinician is operationally defined as one who practices at the highest levels of clinical judgment possible at time and place. These qualifications operationally recognize that clinical judgments may still be more improved by better selection, training and experience opportunities within the limits of what is humanly possible at time and place. Operationally, clinical judgments reflect basic science orientations (the cultural value system against which professional clinicians operate). It is assumed that the clinician is thoroughly grounded in basic science knowledge and in the most up-to-date use of established clinical methods.

This somewhat lengthy quote has special relevance to Chapter Nine that deals with expert testimony.

The contribution of human qualities gets translated into two types of reliability: *intra-judge reliability* and *inter-judge reliability* (note that the term "judge" is used herein, unless clearly stated to the contrary, in a non-legal sense, although it could feasibly apply to court judges). Stated briefly, intra-judge reliability refers to the ability of a single judge to reproduce the exact same judgment, and inter-judge reliability refers to the amount of agreement between two or more judges (Woody, 1972). An example of intra-judge reliability would be that in which a psychiatrist, having been asked to conduct a psychiatric status examination for the court, produces exactly the same diagnosis for the same client on two different occasions (a necessary assumption would be that he did not recall his previous judgment about the client and that the psychiatric data available for him were the same in both examinations). An example of inter-judge reliability, and one that is especially pertinent when expert testimony is involved is judicial proceedings for mentally ill and mentally retarded persons, would pose the question whether two or more psychiatrists, having been asked to conduct a psychiatric status examination for the court and having the same psychiatric data available to them for consideration, would agree on a diagnosis and related aspects of psychiatric status.

## IMPLICATIONS

The foregoing discussion is designed to clarify the basic concept of reliability and to focus attention on the potential vulnerability of human judgment. Although the ensuing chapters will further illustrate how reliability plays an integral role in law in general and in the legal processes for mentally retarded persons in specific, it seems appropriate to highlight the implications of the concept of reliability.

Foremost, of course, is that the constitutional right to equality is predicated on reliable treatment of each individual, regardless of any idiosyncratic characteristic. This somewhat esoteric framework gets translated in everyday activities in a variety of ways. Among others, it is relevant to assuring each person that the decisions, opinions, or judgments formulated about him by persons of recognized authority are not biased. Stated simply, the pronouncements of any authority, regardless of societal system (e.g. legal, educational, medical, etc.), must be objectively derived from valid criteria (i.e. the rationale must be based on more than personal preference) and must be consistent with comparable pronouncements from other authorities.

The theme interlaced throughout this book and culminated as the central message in Chapter Ten is that *all persons dealing with the mentally retarded must be prepared to take responsible actions.* This means that family members and friends, the general public, the members of the "helping professions," and the personnel within the legal system must be prepared, able, and willing both to implement the concept of reliability in their own functions and to assume a "watch-dog" stance to assure that others dealing with the mentally retarded are likewise properly mindful of providing reliable (and, of course, valid) services.

## CHAPTER TWO

# DEFINITION OF MENTAL RETARDATION: A STUDY IN AMBIGUITY

THE PROVISION of any kind of professional service or the establishment of an effective service system is dependent upon being able to delineate the criteria for eligibility or the type of persons to be encompassed. This delineation is also fundamental to assuring *reliable* treatment of any kind, because there must be agreement, based on established objective definition points, as to who may be service recipients and for what kind of intervention.

In the case of the mentally retarded entering into a societally-based service system—whether it be the legal system, the educational system, the medical system, or otherwise—the need for a definition is critical. Although possibly no more critical than for any other type of "deviant" or "exceptional" person, the mentally retarded person does have, from a historical vantage point, a strikingly wide variety of definitions that have been applied to his type of exceptionality.

### PAST DEFINITIONS

The search for a definition via the historical route finds much reference material in what may now be considered a "classic" in mental retardation publications, namely Sarason's (1959) *Psychological Problems in Mental Deficiency*. Among other things, Sarason points out that probably the foremost criterion (and thus definition) of mental retardation is the *intelligence quotient* (IQ) and that, for some reason, the early heavy reliance on this criterion/definition (meaning that scoring in a particular IQ range determines the existence of a type or degree of mental retardation) "seems to have been largely an American phenomenon." This rather primitive assumption, i.e. that a particular IQ is indicative of a specific degree of mental retardation, must be quickly rejected. To summarize his review of research on this issue, Sarason (1959) states:

> It cannot be emphasized too strongly that a low IQ score does not enable one to state in what ways a particular individual is different from others with an identical score, what his differential reactions are to a variety of situations, his attitudes toward himself and others, what effects he will produce on what kinds of people in what kinds of situations, and the relation of the foregoing not only to the presence or absence of central nervous system impairment but to the familial-cultural background in which he developed as well. It is extremely simple, although logically naive, to "explain" a defective child's behavior on the basis of his low IQ—as if there were in the child a force varying inversely with the IQ, "causing" him to behave as he does.

And in so putting asunder the use of the IQ as a singular criterion/definition, Sarason is also, in a sense, prescribing what should be the definition. Other reasons why the singular IQ is not adequate for a definition will emerge from numerous examples in this and subsequent chapters. Regrettably, the IQ has all too often been and remains the singular or most heavily weighted factor in determining, i.e. diagnosing, mental retardation, although the majority of astute professionals do not endorse this practice.

Moving away from the Americanized dependence on the intelligence quotient, the Mental Deficiency Act of 1913 in England (and its subsequent revisions) gave emphasis to a criterion of *social adequacy*. Using the term of the time, *amentia,* Tredgold (7) defined it as: ". . . a state of incomplete mental development of such a kind and degree that the individual is incapable of adapting himself to the normal environment of his fellows in such a way as to maintain existence independently of supervision, control, or external support."

In addition to the emphasis on social adequacy in general, it is significant that Tredgold's definition, using the phrase "incapable of adapting himself to the *normal* environment of *his fellows*" (italics added), casts the definition of mental retardation into a frame of reference that is imbued with cultural relativity. Although Sarason (1959) sees Tredgold's definition as surpassing the criterion of IQ, he notes: "Tredgold seems unaware that the testing situation is a social situation in which the observed relationships between the nature of the stimulus situation (the test item) and the overt and inferred behavior of the individual are as important as the correctness of the response." Thus Tredgold may have too easily dismissed the value of psychological testing (note, however, that psychological testing was in its infancy, perhaps even in its embryonic state, at this point in history). Sarason further states: "It seems clear that for Tredgold the criterion of mental deficiency is the inability to adapt to the "normal" environment of one's "fellows." Such a criterion, by its ambiguity, involves setting up additional criteria of a 'normal environment,' criteria which Tredgold does not present."

In conclusion, Sarason notes that a "more general criticism of Tredgold's approach is that he does not present a theory of behavior development from which deductions may be made and tested so that one may determine how much weight to attach to what factors in understanding an individual's development."

Historically, another major definition was offered by Doll (1941). He set forth six inclusive criteria that he believed were "essential" to an adequate definition of and conceptual understanding of mental deficiency. These criteria were: (1) social incompetence, (2) due to mental subnormality, (3) which has been developmentally arrested, (4) which obtains at maturity, (5) is of constitutional origin, and (6) is essentially incurable. Suffice it to say that the criteria seem an advance beyond the singular criterion notion inherent to intelligence testing and beyond the hyperrelativity and ambiguity of Tredgold's definition, but they fail to differentiate etiological considerations and essentially negate any prognosis for change.

As has been no doubt noted, various terms have been used at different points in time to denote the generic mental retardation status and, in some instances, to specify degrees of mental retardation. For the most part, these terms have not been consistently applied and have often provided more of a lexical game than a contribution to understanding mental retardation. For example, at varying points, amentia, mental deficiency, and mental retardation have been used as the generic term; and, at one point, the term mental retardation was considered all-encompassing, with the two terms, mentally handicapped and mentally deficient, respectively indicating the educable retarded and the custodial-trainable retarded ranges. As mentioned previously in the Preface, no distinction will be made herein between the terminologies *per se;* rather, the term mental retardation is intended to serve a generic purpose, with any subcategorization or delineation being based on functional descriptions instead of terms.

## CONTEMPORARY DEFINITIONS

The evolution of terminologies, diagnostic criteria, and definitions for mental retardation is far from thorough and complete. There has been, however, considerable advancement and sophistication. Whether the "state of the art" is adequate to earn the phrase "state of the *science*" will be discussed in the next section of this chapter. At this point, it seems appropriate to present some of the most relevant contemporary definitions.

As an abbreviated introduction, Stevens (1964) points out: "Mental retardation is a constellation of syndromes. It is not a disease, although it may be the result of a disease." With this brief preface, definitions from the two most authoritative professional sources on mental retardation, the American Psychiatric Association and the American Association on Mental Deficiency, should be considered. The definition endorsed by the American Psychiatric Association states: "Mental retardation refers to subnormal general intellectual functioning which originates during the developmental period and is associated with impairment of either learning and social adjustment or maturation, or both." (American Psychiatric Association, 1968.)

A variety of "clinical subcategories of mental retardation" is provided, and the impression is that more emphasis is placed on organic factors than might be true of other professional organizations. The definition adopted by the American Association on Mental Deficiency states: *"Mental retardation refers to subaverage general intellectual functioning which originates during the developmental period and is associated with impairment in adaptive behavior."* (Heber, 1961.)

In comparing the definitions from the American Psychiatric Association and the American Association on Mental Deficiency, it would appear that, as contrasted to the former, the latter tends to place less emphasis on organic factors *per se* (albeit that they are not necessarily discounted) and tends to emphasize adaptive social behavior, which may be interpreted as suggesting potential for improvement.

In view of the prestigious nature of both the American Psychiatric Association and the American Association on Mental Deficiency and the fact that the latter group represents what is undoubtedly a significant portion of professionals who work with mentally retarded persons, it would seem that their "endorsed" definitions would receive widespread acceptance and practical application. Such may well be the case, but professional publications do include a number of dissenting views, many of which seem to recognize the ambiguity within the definitions. As two examples: Jaslow and Smith (1972) believe that the definition from the American Association on Mental Deficiency should describe the problems that the person has, rather than describing the nature of the person; and McAllister (1972) prefers to take issue with reflections on both the person and the problems, and instead, to emphasize modification of adaptive behavior:

> After all, once the person with mental retardation problems correctly interprets the environment and starts making correct or adaptive responses, he appears less likely to return to nonadaptive or incorrect functioning than the person who does not have these problems. Mental retardation simply refers to the problems certain people have in modifying behavioral patterns in accord with the consequences of their responses. It is logically possible that changes in methodologies of teaching, for example, can modify certain of these patterns. The state of the art in this area could in no way be considered advanced at present.

The foregoing should illustrate that professionals lack cohesion in their attempts at defining mental retardation, not to mention the fact, as will be noted in the following paragraphs, that the definitions available provide little definitiveness for professional services.

## RELIABILITY AND DEFINITION

As the review of definitions has illustrated, there is no one definition available that unquestionably distinguishes the so-called mentally retarded condition. Thus attaining reliability in services for the mentally retarded, regardless of the societally-based service system, is somewhat hampered (and possibly even "doomed for failure" unless proper precautions are taken) because of the problems surrounding the definition.

Before concentrating on the issues inherent to defining mental retardation, it should be noted that the condition of mental retardation itself may contribute to poor reliability (even if an adequate definition could be adopted). Sarason (1959) notes: "The present-day status of the psychological sciences does not allow one to consider predictions about future status and amenability to environmental change as other than tentative and subject to much error"; and the "status of the psychological sciences" has not changed that much since Sarason made that comment more than a decade ago. Further, Sarason points out an important measurement issue relevant to the mentally retarded when he states: "It should be noted at this point that the reliability and validity of a diagnosis of mental deficiency increase as the intellectual level of the individual decreases." What this means is two-fold. First, the lower a person's intellectual functioning falls in the mentally retarded range, the more likely it is that his adaptation, intellect, and functioning will remain approximately the same (unless, of course, some highly efficacious therapeutic-educational interventions were made, as will be discussed in Chapter Ten). Second, the nature of psychological tests (particularly intelligence tests) are loaded in favor of verbal and language skills, skills that increase many performances necessary for psychological measures. Such skills can be optimally manifested in the testing situation with persons in the upper limits of the mentally retarded range.

The variations in definitions and the nebulous nature of definitions have frustrated some professionals as they recognize the extreme ambiguity that is operational whenever the diagnosis of mental retardation must be made. Consider the following statement: "Anyone who has tried to establish a medical diagnosis of mentally retarded individuals knows what frustration is. The clinician continually encounters individuals who presumably fit a diagnosis of which he (or she) is not aware—perhaps a disease already delineated, perhaps not. So many syndromes and diseases have been described that no one can remember them all, nor would there be any point in trying." (Holmes, Moser, Halldorsson, Mack, Pant, and Matzilevich, 1972.) Parenthetically, the likelihood of poor reliability is great because of the inability of the human mind to remember seemingly countless "syndromes and diseases."

Further, in an exhaustive review of cross-cultural epidemiological studies, Gruenberg (1964) was left essentially unable to draw meaningful comparisons, partly because of the methodological difficulties in this kind of research and partly because of the unique defining qualities given to mental retardation in different cultures: "The data in the section of this chapter on community diagnosis show that the reliability of techniques for doing community surveys is not sufficiently developed at the present time to make long-range, repeated measurements of the prevalence of all forms of mental retardation. In order to make such measurements one must have some set of criteria which can be used repeatedly over a prolonged period of time." (Gruenberg, 1964.)

And he adds: "The definitions of, diagnostic criteria for, and administrative modes of recording cases of mental retardation do not promise to become sufficiently stabilized in the near future to provide us with a clear picture." The difficulty in establishing a universal definition of mental retardation is obviously dependent upon cultural differences and dependent on the means by which different cultures deal with persons who are other than "normal."

Another major barrier to an agreed upon definition is, logically, the symptoms or signs of mental retardation. As mentioned, cultures differ in what they believe the signs to be. Further, even signs that receive relative agreement between professionals are sometimes evasive of detection (Sarason, 1959). And finally, mental retardation is not a mutually exclusive set of signs; that is, the signs that are presumed to reflect mental retardation may also be found in non-mentally retarded persons. In regard to the latter, it is easy to find contradictions within the professional research literature regarding signs that presumably reflect a particular clinical condition; for example, there are signs (i.e. observable behaviors) that some professionals would interpret as reflecting mental retardation, others would interpret as reflecting brain injury or the hyperkinetic syndrome, and others would interpret as reflecting emotional disturbance (Woody, 1969). The frightening thing is that many of these hallowed signs, such as those for detecting the hyperkinetic behavioral syndrome and the manifestations of brain injury or perceptual impairment, have apparently been erroneously promulgated and have achieved "mythological validity," and when these signs are subjected to experimental investigation, they have occasionally proven to be false (Browning, 1967; Woody, 1969).

Another issue that deserves recognition is that "mental retardation" is all too frequently grouped with "mental illness," particularly in legal definitions. For example, Bray (1971) describes the Australian Mental Health Act and points out how many common law practices are directed at the "mentally defective" person. The "mentally defective" person, as might be anticipated, encompasses the mentally ill *and* the intellectually retarded. Although somewhat of a digression from the principal point, it might be worth noting the Australian Mental Health Act definitions; Bray (1971) defines a "mentally defective" person: "(a) a person who is mentally ill, that is to say a person who owing to his mental condition requires oversight care or control for his own good or in the public interest, and who owing to disorder of the mind or mental infirmity arising from age or the decay of his faculties is incapable of managing himself or his affairs, or (b) an intellectually retarded person. 'Intellectually retarded' means suffering from an arrested or incomplete development of mind including subnormality of intelligence of a nature or degree which requires or is susceptible to medical treatment or other specialized care or training."

Aside from what might be the questionable adequacy (in

terms of specificity) of these two definitions and the fact that, theoretically, a mentally retarded person might well possess some of the characteristics deemed to be within the "mentally ill" definition, e.g. incapable of self-management (and thus might be erroneously labeled "mentally ill"), this legal definition readily reveals why certain law processes, such as common law, may treat the mentally retarded person in an unreliable (indeed, perhaps even invalid) manner. Incidentally, there are repeated examples within legal publications of the combining of mental illness and mental retardation; and the combination often leads to an illogical blending of the legal processes for the two groups of persons. For example, a review of tort liability by Curran (1960) to be cited subsequently, while being extremely authoritative, still considers the mentally ill and the mentally retarded together.

Perhaps the most noteworthy issue within the definitions of mental retardation is that unequivocal criteria for presence or absence of mental retardation are not provided. Therefore, there is ample opportunity for subjectivity, which means, in the case of legal processes for the mentally retarded, the clinical judgments that go into expert testimony or into decisions by both a jury and a judge are left with an indeterminable degree of latitude. As will become even more evident in Chapter Three, dealing with diagnostic procedures, the definition of the condition, in this case mental retardation, is critical to the diagnostic processes; for example, Benton (1964) states: "In clinical work, diagnostic practice is dependent upon, and, in large measure, determined by, prevailing theoretical assumptions about the nature of mental retardation. Thus the decision, on the basis of a psychological evaluation, that a given individual is or is not mentally retarded ultimately depends as much on the clinician's fundamental conception of the nature of mental retardation as it does on the specific findings of the examination."

Since the definition of mental retardation is in an ambiguous state of affairs (which may be an understatement) and since there appears to be a relationship between an examiner's conceptualization, i.e. definition, of mental retardation and his diagnosis—and the latter has been documented with a large number of studies for emotionally disturbed as well as mentally retarded persons cited elsewhere (Woody and Woody, 1972)—it seems justified to assert: *The failure to establish a definition of mental retardation, one which encompasses objectively measurable diagnostic criteria, contributes negatively to the quest for a respectable level of reliability in legal processes for the mentally retarded.* Thus, the usage of definitions of mental retardation must still be viewed as the "state of the *art*," and not as the "state of the *science*."

The failure to agree on a universal definition of mental retardation and the undeniable factors that counteract reliable services in any relevant societally-based service system must not be allowed to serve as a rationale for rejecting involvement with mental retardation. Likewise, such conditions cannot be allowed to cast a pall over concern for helping mentally retarded persons. Although reality and although less than ideal, these conditions should be interpreted as a stimulus for more effective actions. This same constructive, action-oriented stance must pervade the subsequent chapters, particularly Chapter Three on diagnosis and Chapter Four on nosological/classification systems; these next two chapters are closely related to the issue of definition.

## CHAPTER THREE

# DIAGNOSTIC PRACTICES IN LEGAL PROCEEDINGS FOR THE MENTALLY RETARDED

IMPLICIT TO THE ENTIRE SCOPE of legal proceedings is the assumption that judgments will be made, and in the case of legal proceedings involving a "mental condition" (be it under the rubric of mental illness or mental retardation) is the assumption that some form of *expert* judgment will be rendered. Typically this would be conceptualized as a mental health professional making an appraisal, with the concomitant formulation of "expert opinions," and offering specialized information via his testimony as a contribution to the legal proceedings. The most rudimentary description of the mental health professional's actions in this context can be summarized into one critical word: *diagnosis.*

As will emerge in the ensuing discussion, the term "diagnosis" is not a simple concept; a composite of parameters must be fulfilled if the term is to be justly applied. This chapter focuses on defining the term "diagnosis" (i.e. specifying its perimeter and its multi-faceted nature), in order to fit the theoretical concept that underlies diagnosis into the context of legal proceedings, and to describe the diagnostic practices that are manifested in legal proceedings, particularly as applicable to mentally retarded persons.

## DEFINING DIAGNOSIS

Diagnosis is a process. Thorne (1961) describes diagnosis as a problem-solving process; that is, the judge is exposed to "a mass of discrete data and required to organize it in meaningful ways" in order that he can find solutions to specific questions (such as: Is the person normal or abnormal?). On a more simplistic level,

Arbuckle (1965) defines diagnosis in the context of counseling and psychotherapy: "Diagnosis may be considered as the analysis of one's difficulties and the causes that have produced them. More clinically, it may be thought of as the determination of the nature, origin, precipitation and maintenance of ineffective abnormal modes of behavior. More simply, it may be considered as the development by the counselor, of a deeper and more accurate understanding and appreciation of the client."

What should be emerging from this discussion of the term "diagnosis" is that there are numerous facets: *diagnosis is a multifaceted process.* Beller (1962) presents the linkage of facets as: "observation, description, a delineation of causation or etiology, classification, prediction or prognosis, and control-modification or treatment plan." Woody (1969) summarizes the facets into three phases, all of which are required in order to fulfill the definition for the term "diagnosis": *"The present functioning or characteristics should be evaluated and described; possible causative factors or etiology should be posited; and a prognosis should be made and a treatment approach recommended."*

The foregoing definitions of "diagnosis" reveal that the term requires more than merely determining that a person is functioning at a particular level, whether the factor in question be a dimension of personality or be an intellectual level. In the case of the mentally retarded, therefore, practices within many legal cases involving mentally retarded persons do not, in fact, fulfill the criteria for diagnosis. In other words, all too frequently the alleged mentally retarded person is administered an intelligence test and even though the test itself may be valid and reliable, the resulting data are simply intelligence quotients or the scaled scores for the subtests within the intelligence test. The so-called "diagnosis" does provide some evidence relevant to "present functioning and characteristics," but there is seldom an attempt to try to delineate "possible causative factors or etiology"; moreover, there is virtually never "a prognosis" offered. In the broadest sense, it might be claimed that the decision to place the person in a state institution for the mentally retarded is a prognostic step, but at best this would seem to be an expedient administrative action that only vaguely relates to the actual intent of the prognostic facet of the definition of diagnosis. Adequate diagnosis involves several critical facets that are often by-passed in the case of mentally retarded persons; one such critical facet is the prognostic recommendation: "Thus a diagnosis of any sort should be viewed as having limited value if it does not lead to a recommendation for an intervention. There might well be instances where the outcome of an evaluation would lead to a recommendation of no therapy or treatment, but even no treatment can be viewed as an intervention, i.e. the regular environmental circumstances are allowed to occur without interruption." (Woody, 1972.)

And continuing to the important point: "Essentially, the process is one of stating the estimates and assumptions about the person and then postulating what would happen if they were afforded each of several possible treatment modes." (Woody, 1972.)

Thorne (1961) attaches the term "etiologic equation" to this procedure. The critical point is that diagnosis involves a weighing of alternative interventions, and it may be asserted that the "diagnostic services" typically afforded to the mentally retarded person (if, indeed, any are afforded at all) do not deal with the etiological and the prognostic facets. They deal only with the description of the present functioning, and this is commonly done only in the very rudimentary framework of a statement of intelligence quotient.

Thus from the professional psychologist's point of view, the "diagnostic" services within the legal processes for the mentally retarded frequently fail to meet the standards of an adequate diagnosis and could be more aptly termed "labeling." The remainder of this chapter will be based on the definition of "diagnostics" most commonly encountered in legal proceedings for the mentally retarded, albeit not always an adequate definition of diagnosis when manifested in legal proceedings.

## THE CONCEPT OF DIAGNOSIS IN LEGAL PROCEEDINGS

For the context of this discussion on legal proceedings, a generic definition of diagnosis will be used. Admittedly, this may result in the grouping of rather diverse diagnostic "bed-fellows," e.g. encompassing the psychiatric examination for insanity defense purposes and the intellectual testing for certification of mental retardation for purposes of institutionalization.

The introduction into legal proceedings of the factor called "mental condition" must be scrutinized. The Harvard Law Review Association (1970) indicates that there are two ways mental condition can be introduced; the first regards the accused's competency to stand trial and the second regards whether he can be held criminally responsible for the acts with which he is charged. Surrounding these two possibilities, there has been much debate on the constitutionality of examinations relevant to eliciting information that would establish that the accused committed the act with which he is charged. As an example, one might question the requirement that an alleged mentally retarded person should take an intelligence test in an involuntary commitment case. The Harvard Law Review Association (1970) notes that a few courts have declared the psychiatric examination unconstitutional or have not allowed the use of information elicited in the examination that would establish the commitment of the act, but there is not final agreement on this issue: "Although several courts have considered the constitutionality of forcing a defendant to reveal information about his mental state, none has found the process impermissible *per se*. Most of the decisions upholding examination requirements predated the Supreme Court's ruling that the federal constitutional privilege against self-incrimination applies to the states."

The review focuses on: ". . . first, whether in a psychiatric examination the type of information elicited, and the means used fall within the privileged area; second, whether incrimination results from the use of the information on the question of sanity or competency; and third, whether a waiver of the privilege should be implied when the defendant puts his doctors on the stand."

It is noted that the court has failed to "give guidelines for striking the balance between truth seeking and the values of the privilege."

## DIAGNOSTIC PRACTICES

At the point of entering into consideration of the diagnostic procedures used in mental retardation, it is necessary to reintroduce a term that was cited in Chapter One: *Validity*. As will be recalled, without validity, the highest reliability means nothing. Masland, Sarason, and Gladwin (1958) state:

> One fact does stand out prominently, however, and that is that the criteria customarily used to define mental retardation are not adequate to predict social and occupational success and failure except at the extremes. We are fairly safe in predicting that even a borderline case will never reach the higher categories of professional-intellectual status, and we can be reasonably certain that a severely retarded individual will never be able to function fully independently in society. Several lines of evidence support this conclusion.

As was elaborated upon previously (see Chapter Two), definitions of "mental retardation" *per se* are not always consistent and there are few, if any, definitive criteria that would lead to a valid set toward mental retardation. Robinson and Robinson (1965) comment on the validity of the diagnostic task:

> For the psychodiagnostician whose principal task it is to investigate the child's psychological behavior, however, this approach to diagnosis is not satisfactory. As yet, there are practically no known test patterns based on physiological or psychological etiology which can be said to be certainly diagnostic of any given underlying condition. There is some hint that focalized lesions in the brain may produce characteristic test behaviors in children and adults, but these behaviors are not found exclusively in brain-injured individuals and thus are of little help in diagnosis.

Robitscher (1966) quotes a report from the American Bar Foundation that indicates that the psychiatrist's inability to ascertain accurately the capacity to distinguish right from wrong through (presumably) valid medical criteria leads to his testimony being "largely conjecture or a reflection of his own personal judgments of whether or not the defendant should be held responsible." While this statement is directed to the discussion on criminal liability, it also illustrates that, aside from the questionable reliability that might result, there is a sparsity of known valid criteria for a variety of expert judgments made in legal contexts. Parenthetically, the thoroughness of the examination has distinct ramifications for both the validity and reliability concepts, and it is not unusual that a client's socioeconomic status or limited available resources result in abbreviated examinations. Chambers (1972) notes ". . . the examination process was far less thorough than the doctors themselves considered satisfactory."

With regard to legal proceedings, the primary method for evaluating persons thought to be mentally retarded is, of course, intelligence testing. Hutt and Gibby (1965) state:

> A number of basic assumptions underlie all intelligence testing, and we should become familiar with them in order to understand the values and limitations of all intelligence tests. Whenever a child is given an intelligence test it is assumed that he has had the background and experiences suitable to the test that is employed. (For example, a test that is dependent upon language functions cannot be given to a child who has not had an adequate background in such language functions.) Further, it must be assumed that the test is given and scored by an examiner who has been adequately trained in the administration and interpretation of the test. Another basic assumption is that the child functions on the test in a manner that is indicative of his true capacities. This implies that the child is adequately motivated to take the test, is cooperative in the test situation, is not unduly anxious, and is not physically incapable of responding minimally to the test items.

Relatedly, Masland, Sarason, and Gladwin (1958) note that: "Undoubtedly motivational factors, subcultural and individual, play a major role in precipitating mental retardation and deserve careful attention in assessing individual cases."

There is, therefore, a strong influence from cultural conditions, and it should be apparent that certain mentally retarded persons, because of the cultural conditions to which they have been exposed during their development, would—in all likelihood—perform on an intelligence test in a manner that would not, in fact, measure their true mental functioning. Further, there are personality or emotional factors (e.g. anxiety that might be evoked by the person's being placed in an evaluative setting) that would adversely influence the testing outcome. As but one example, Woody and Billy (1970) conducted a study which divided retarded and non-retarded boys into experimental and control groups. All were administered an intelligence test, and all were to be involved in retesting. However, in the retesting nothing special was done with the control groups, but the experimental subjects were given suggestions designed to facilitate rapport, induce physical relaxation, lower possible anxiety over past test performance, and establish motivation and a pretest set of positive expectations for the retesting (with an alternate form of the intelligence test). Although there were limitations imposed by the research design, it was found that the non-retarded subjects, regardless of whether they did or did not receive suggestions, did not make significant change on the post-testing, but that the experimental mentally retarded subjects (those who received the aforementioned suggestions) did, in fact, attain a statistically significant increase in their mean intelligence quotient over the mean intelligence quotient for the control mentally retarded subjects (those who received no suggestions). While not definitive in itself, this study points toward the possibility that psychological, socio-cultural, and emotional factors lead to lowered, i.e. invalid and unreliable, intelligence measures with mentally retarded persons and that these factors might be counteracted successfully by therapeutic techniques, such as clinical suggestions and special efforts to create an optimal positive relationship/contextual set for the evaluation. To summarize, both reliability and validity can easily be affected by cultural and personal factors.

As mentioned in the discussion on the reliability concept in Chapter One, there are statistical properties within essentially every test that would lead to some variance being expected, i.e. variance between a test/retest set of scores because of the test itself, not because of the person's characteristics. Without belaboring the point, intelligence tests, even the most sophisticated ones (such as those in the Wechsler series and the Stanford-Binet), are no exceptions.

Within legal and penal contexts, it is difficult to sort out exactly what are the factors that lead to the inconsistency in test results. Some of the inconsistency may be due to the statistical properties inherent to the test construction and some of the inconsistency may be due to the environmental or contextual conditions (e.g. being tested in a prison as opposed to being tested in a plush office of a private practitioner).

There are two studies, which will be discussed further in Chapter Five, where retesting led to quite different mean intelligence quotients: Brown and Courtless (1968), in a study of fifty prisoners, found that retesting resulted in only 75 percent of them continuing to be in the retarded category (with another 9% in the borderline category), i.e. there were approximately 16 percent who clearly moved beyond the mentally retarded category in the retesting; and Brown, Courtless, and Silber (1970), in a study of 56 mentally retarded offenders, found that the retesting left only 64 percent in the same retarded category, i.e. approximately 36 percent moved into the non-retarded category in the retesting. In a similar manner, Allen (1968) took a group of prisoners who had a mean intelligence quotient of 61.8 on the Otis Test of Mental Ability; they were retested with the Wechsler Adult Intelligence Scale, and they earned a mean intelligence quotient of 77.8 (with only one person being below a 70 IQ). This seems to illustrate how intelligence tests, both of which in this case are quite respectable test instruments in terms of psychometric standards, can lead to significantly different results. In other words, the choice of the test will be influential in the diagnosis of the mentally retarded person, and it may be speculated that the choice of a different second test could lead to a significantly different intelligence measure. This is, quite obviously, poor diagnostic reliability.

Levy (1965) made an empirical survey of the state guardianship system in Minnesota, and in so doing uncovered a variety of diagnostic practices relevant to the mentally retarded that were, to say the least, appalling. He cites a case of a man committed to guardianship in 1929 who did not test below "dull normal" from 1949 to 1960, but was still placed in the Annex for Defective Delinquents and went without judicial review throughout this period; this is comparable to several other cases cited, such as a case of a boy who, though never diagnosed as being mentally retarded, was kept for several years in an institution for the mentally retarded. He notes that at one time, in the 1920's, it was maintained that "obvious feeble-mindedness" could be proved by: "(1) physical appearance; (2) opinions of relatives; (3) opinion in community; and (4) observations on the acquisition and ability to do the ordinary things of everyday life, which may in part be tested directly on the child."

It should be noted that this view was expressed by a "noted intelligence authority," Dr. Fred Kuhlman, in a statement to probate judges. Aside from the obvious lack of validity and specificity within these so-called "authoritative criteria," it should go without question that the determination of any and all of these criteria are highly valuable and are subject to personal biases—they are, therefore, lacking in characteristics that would adequately assure reliable judgments. Fortunately, those were applied some fifty years ago—but have conditions substantially changed?

False criteria, unfortunately, still continue. As cited in the preceding definition, "physical appearance" was considered. Although not the sole basis for decision (hopefully), Kay, Farnham, Karren, Knakal, and Diamond (1972) note that: "Although most of the judges recognize their inability to diagnose a person as mentally retarded, some judges found reassuring confirmation of the medical diagnosis in the physical appearance of the most profoundly retarded persons." Perhaps the state of affairs has not changed entirely in the last fifty years!

Levy (1965) seems especially critical of intelligence test reliability. He presents evidence of significantly different serial intelligence measures (i.e. intelligence measures made on the same person in a longitudinal fashion), and states that the lack of reliability is due to: ". . . socio-cultural factors, reading handicaps, anxiety caused by the testing situation, and emotional instability."

Another major issue, which relates to both reliability and validity, is the "expert" who makes a diagnosis; more will be said about this matter in Chapter Nine on expert testimony. Two examples should suffice for the present. First, there are professionals who devise their own "tests," but who never go to the trouble to statistically document their tests' reliability and validity. As one seemingly infamous example, Levy (1965) describes a psychiatrist who claimed to "specialize in IQ tests" (incidentally, training in the administration of psychological tests is not part of the typical psychiatric training curriculum and apparently there was no evidence that this particular psychiatrist had ever received formal academic training for his professed "specialization"), and Levy (1965) states: "In fact, this psychiatrist specializes (without training) in 10 minute oral examinations—with questions apparently derived from a Stanford-Binet primer." Within this example are, of course, ethical questions, but more importantly for this discussion of diagnostic services to the mentally retarded, it illustrates how a professional, protected by his academic degreed-stature, may still resort to an evaluation procedure (in this instance it would seemingly be better to label it a "pseudo-evaluation procedure") that seems highly likely to be both poor in validity and low in inter-judge reliability (from a professional vantage point it might be more appropriate to use the stronger terminology of being "invalid" and "unreliable"). The second example is that legal systems sometimes accept "expert opinions" from persons who are, in fact, not expert in the particular topic but who do possess an esteemed academic degree. Most notorious perhaps has been the practice of allowing physicians who are non-psychiatrists to conduct quasi-psychiatric examinations and to determine commitment to mental hospitals. It seems prudent to say that traditional medical training programs and consequently the majority of (non-psychiatric) physicians are void of academic contents adequate to lead to reliable and, indeed, valid judgments about mental status for psychiatric commitments. Further, the same case is true with mental retardation; expert attestations of mental retardation frequently come from professionals who have had no training in mental retardation *per se*. In Levy's (1965) analysis of Minnesota's system for protecting the mentally retarded, he notes that during the hearing a patient must be examined by two medical doctors and *may* also include a person skilled in the ascertainment of mental deficiency. Murdock (1972), based on the Alabama case *(Wyatt v. Stickney),* quotes a detailed definition for the "Qualified Mental Retardation Professional" (see Murdock, 1972, p. 173) which says, in essence, that *every* member of a professional discipline —psychology, medicine, education, social work, physical/vocational/occupational therapy, and nursing—must have specialized training in and experience with mental retardation before they can rightfully deem themselves to be a "qualified mental retardation professional." Chapter Ten will include further discussion of the need for truly qualified professionals.

Another area relevant to reliability in the diagnosis of mental retardation is the categorization scheme used for IQ groups. There are numerous sources that attach a particular hierarchiacal label to a given IQ range. It seems unnecessary to review these in detail. The most common, at this point in time, is the one endorsed by the American Association on Mental Deficiency (Heber, 1961):

| *Category* | *IQ Range* |
|---|---|
| Borderline | 70-84 |
| Mild | 55-69 |
| Moderate | 40-54 |
| Severe | 25-39 |
| Profound | Below 25 |

The *Wechsler Adult Intelligence Scale Manual* (Wechsler, 1955), disregarding the above-average ranges that are cited, provides the following:

| *Category* | *IQ Range* |
|---|---|
| Average | 90-109 |
| Dull Normal | 80-89 |
| Borderline | 70-79 |
| Mental Defective | 69 and Below |

And as a final example, the American Psychiatric Association's (1968) *Diagnostic and Statistical Manual of Mental Disorders* (2nd ed.) provides the following still different categorization scheme:

| *Category* | *IQ Range* |
|---|---|
| Borderline Mental Retardation | 68-85 |
| Mild Mental Retardation | 52-67 |
| Moderate Mental Retardation | 36-51 |
| Severe Mental Retardation | 20-35 |
| Profound Mental Retardation | Under 20 |

This material could have been included with equal propriety in the following chapter on nosology and classification systems, but it is cited at this point to underscore how the use of a descriptive diagnostic term for mental retardation does not automatically prescribe the IQ range. It is necessary to specify the source of the descriptive terminology, otherwise interpretive reliability will suffer.

## SUMMARY

To briefly summarize this chapter, diagnosis for mentally retarded persons in legal proceedings is frequently an incomplete process. That is, it all too frequently labels or describes current functioning but does not deal with etiology or postulations for optimal treatment—each of which is necessary for "complete" fulfillment of the term "diagnosis." There seems to be some constitutional questions regarding the soliciting or obtaining of information that will be used in the diagnosis of the mentally retarded. Further, there is questionable validity for the commonly held indices of mental retardation, and reliability frequently falters because of idiosyncratic factors entering into the evaluation procedures, e.g. cultural and personality factors, because of illogical professional appraisal practices, because of poor intratest and inter-test consistencies (which occur for a multitude of statistical, environmental, and psychological reasons), and because of differing descriptive terminologies.

## CHAPTER FOUR

# NOSOLOGICAL AND CLASSIFICATION SYSTEMS FOR THE MENTALLY RETARDED

THE PRECEDING CHAPTER on diagnosis has introduced the issue of classification systems for the mentally retarded, particularly in terms of the descriptive terms used to identify a particular range of intelligence quotients. In Chapter Two, reference was also made to the American Psychiatric Association's (1968) classification system, which was viewed as giving more emphasis to organic factors than might be endorsed by less medically oriented groups. This chapter will, therefore, focus on four issues: the need for nosology and classification; the reliability of nosology and classification; generic problems of nosology and classification; and the types of criminal problems, i.e. the nosological categories, found with mentally retarded offenders.

## THE NEED FOR NOSOLOGY AND CLASSIFICATION

The issue of a need for nosology or classification has been subjected to much debate, and the scope of this discussion does not accommodate a resolution. The strongest proponent is unquestionably the American Psychiatric Association which believes that a well defined nosological system will accommodate the collection of vital statistics necessary for social and mental health planning and development, the conducting of epidemiological investigations with world-wide significance for disease control and prevention, the effective development of mental health facilities and programs, and the most efficacious treatment of the individual. On the other extreme, perhaps, are persons (like Thomas S. Szasz) who believe nosology perpetuates medical myths. For example, Szasz (1968) states:

> Although the term "psychiatric nosology" means the classification of psychiatric diseases, modern developments in psychiatry have led to new taxonomic possibilities. This has come about as psychiatry has developed into both a basic science and a set of clinical techniques. It is only as a clinical science that psychiatry is oriented toward diseases, diagnoses, and treatments. As a basic science, psychiatry, like other sciences, is oriented toward a non-judgmental understanding of the phenomena it studies. Taxonomic systems of this type aim at ordering data to increase our sense of clarity, and at helping us master or control our subject matter. Classifications designed solely for the purpose of diagnosis and treatment represent a special type of taxonomic system. When we apply them to other, non-therapeutic (for example, judicial) situations, the results are likely to be disastrous.

Szasz (1968) takes special issue with the concept of insanity; he states:

> In actuality, there are several psychiatric classifications of people and of mental diseases. For example, the distinction between sane and insane is relevant only in a judicial context. Indeed, psychiatrists often protest that these terms have no "medical meaning." Paradoxically, this does not prevent them from offering their services in situations where these terms are used. The point, I think, is not whether the term "insanity" has or has not a medical meaning, but rather that it is relevant only in a legal situation. The adjectives "medical" and "legal" should qualify "situation," not "meaning."

Szasz and Alexander (1972) make strong statements that basically support each person's right to be self-determining, even those who are allegedly incompetent, and seem to be negative toward how the traditional approach of the legal system (and psychiatrists working therein) has dealt with the alleged incompetent's right to property and the assigning of guardianship. The impression is created that Szasz, and presumably his supporting colleagues, believes that nosology, particularly as applied by psychiatrists within our legal system, has more often than not worked against the welfare and rights of the alleged incompetent.

## THE RELIABILITY OF NOSOLOGY AND CLASSIFICATION

The issue of reliability of nosological applications is, of course, central to this entire book. While pages could be filled discussing all of the many ramifications intrinsic to this issue, Livermore, Malmquist, and Meehl (1968) have, through examining the justifications for civil commitment, provided an astute summary statement:

> One need only glance at the diagnostic manual of the American Psychiatric Association to learn what an elastic concept mental illness is. It ranges from the massive functional inhibition characteristics of one form of catatonic schizophrenia to those seemingly slight aberrancies associated with an emotionally unstable personality, but which are so close to conduct in which we all engage as to define the entire continuum involved. Obviously, the definition of mental illness is left largely to the user and is dependent upon the norms of adjustment that he employs. Usually the use of the phrase "mental illness" effectively masks the actual norms being applied. And, because of the unavoidably ambiguous generalities in which the American Psychiatric Association describes its diagnostic categories, the diagnostician has the ability to shoehorn into the mentally diseased class almost any person he wishes, for whatever reason, to put there.

The last sentence of this quote is of paramount importance, saying in effect that a professional could potentially classify anyone as being "mentally diseased." To illustrate the validity of this statement and to demonstrate how simply it can be accomplished, one professor of a graduate-level course in human appraisal requires his doctoral students to, through self-introspection, define their psychological and behavioral characteristics and fit them or "shoehorn" them into one of the American Psychiatric Association's nosological categories. Seldom, if ever, does a student fail to find a "mental disease" that could hypothetically be applied to him, and often they find that they could be fitted into more than one category! And by no means are these students, in fact, "mentally diseased," but it does reveal that the most prestigious nosological system available could lead to very unreliable and invalid "diagnoses."

## GENERIC PROBLEMS OF NOSOLOGY AND CLASSIFICATION

There are a number of problems that can contribute to poor reliability in applying nosological and classification systems for the mentally retarded. In discussing problems in classification of retarded children, Hutt and Gibby (1965) indicate:

> There are, however, many problems inherent in the task of attempting to devise an adequate system of classification. If, for example, we attempt a classification based upon the behavioral reactions of retarded children (like some of the cited systems of classification), we need to take into account the fact that children with the same kinds of behavior or symptoms often have very different underlying problems. In the first place, a symptom may be the result of very different causes or processes.

Continuing, they state: "In the second place, a given form of behavior may have different implications depending upon the way it is used and the personality of the particular child showing the reaction; and the same behavior may have a different significance at different times in the life history of the same person. . . . Therefore, to base a system of classification of mental retardation upon behavioral reactions alone presents many difficulties."

But other alternatives possess shortcomings as well, as Hutt and Gibby (1965) reveal:

> If, on the other hand, we attempt to base a system of classification upon underlying causes or dynamics, our problems are complicated. The same cause may produce different reactions in different people. There is no single cause for an abnormal form of behavior; causation is complex. . . . It is also unsatisfactory to base a system of classification entirely upon the results of intelligence test performance. To do so would be to assume that the results of such a test are entirely valid manifestations of intellectual capacity, and that other factors need not be considered. Such an assumption would not be true.

Hutt and Gibby (1965) take the summary position that no system of classification of mentally retarded children is completely adequate and that the systems are rather crude attempts to classify an entity, i.e. mental retardation, that is inadequately understood. This view would support that, with the lack of an adequate classification system, it is premature to expect that the professional practitioner could enter into classification activities in a reliable fashion.

But there is another problem area that is of probably equal significance: the influence of personal/professional characteristics. Social psychological research has found that the socioeconomic background of the professional influences significantly his judgmental functioning. In studying psychologists and psychiatrists, Mitchell and Namenek (1970) found a significant relationship between the therapist's socioeconomic background and the social class of his typical client, i.e. the therapists with lower class backgrounds usually served more lower class patients than those therapists with middle and upper class backgrounds. Relatedly, Rowden, Michel, Dillehay, and Martin (1970) had psychological and psychiatric trainees analyze extensive mental health data for a group of patients and had them rank each patient for suitability for psychotherapy; a positive relationship between social class and recommendations for psychotherapy was found, i.e. the higher the patient's social class, the more likely he would be recommended for psychotherapy. In a study of the influence of the espoused theory of psychotherapy among psychiatrists, Pasamanick, Dinitz, and Lefton (1959) demonstrated that the treatment theory endorsed by the diagnostician had a distinct influence on the psychiatric diagnosis: "It was discerned that the greater the commitment to an analytic orientation, the less the inclination toward diagnosing patients as schizophrenics." And in a study of the influence of the professional status of one's colleagues, Temerlin (1970) found that mental health professionals and nonprofessionals in a community mental health program tended to diagnose a healthy man (his health had been ascertained by a variety of criteria) as being "mentally ill" after they heard a high status, renowned mental health professional (who was serving as a confederate for the research project) characterize the pseudo-patient as being psychotic. These kinds of experimental studies strongly support the conclusion that expert judgments regarding diagnosis and the application of nosological and classification systems are vulnerable to influences from a multiplicity of sources, and that respectable reliability can in no way be assumed.

## THE NOSOLOGICAL CATEGORIES FOUND WITH MENTALLY RETARDED OFFENDERS

A final area in nosological and classification systems for the mentally retarded is the types of crimes with which mentally retarded offenders become involved. An exhaustive review of the research literature would not be in keeping with the overall objectives of this treatise, but two highly relevant studies should provide some exemplary data.

Brown and Courtless (1968) studied penal and correctional institutions for purposes of identifying how mentally retarded criminals were handled. When asked about the primary crimes for which mentally retarded persons had been convicted and had been sentenced to their institutions, the data indicated that 38 percent of the respondents ranked breaking and entering and burglary as the crimes most committed by the retarded. When considering inmates with an intelligence quotient below 55, 57 percent of the inmates were imprisoned for crimes against persons (e.g. homicide, assault, and sexual offenses); it should be noted that 27 percent of the prison population were imprisoned for these offenses. Regarding criminal homicide, 15 percent of the inmates with an intelligence quotient below 55 were imprisoned for this reason, whereas 5.1 percent of the total prison population were imprisoned for this reason. Brown and Courtless (1968) provide other data that are of interest to this issue, but suffice it to say that the foregoing data indicate that a "conviction nosological system" might merit special attention for mentally retarded criminals.

In what is essentially an epidemiological study of the "mentally abnormal offender" in England, Rollin (1969) placed virtually none of the subjects (or an imperceptible percentage) in the "subnormal" category in his comparative profile of clinical diagnoses for offenders and nonoffenders. The large majority of the mentally abnormal offenders were labeled "schizophrenic," which could conceivably encompass some mentally retarded persons; but apparently the mental retardation, if present, was not considered to be the *primary* mental deviancy. Because of the seemingly non-existent status of mental retardation in the group offenders, this rather detailed and extensive study did not attribute any type of crime to or place any categorization scheme onto the mentally retarded.

It must be acknowledged that it is almost impossible (at least practically speaking) to obtain an accurate set of statistics on the relationship between mental retardation and criminality. Although there are numerous reasons, ranging from cultural to methodological factors, one of the foremost reasons is that some court systems are highly cognizant of mental retardation, albeit this is seemingly the exception rather than the rule. In these instances, the mentally retarded person who has allegedly committed a crime is frequently channeled, such as by the judge, directly into the mental health/mental retardation service system, rather than into the legal system. For example, in a case of a young man accused of sodomy, the judge sought a psychological evaluation from a consulting psychologist, involved a social worker, and promptly moved him toward involuntary commitment to a state institution for the mentally retarded, as opposed to subjecting him to criminal proceedings which would have, in all likelihood, led to his being sentenced to prison (his brother, who was involved in the same act with him was subsequently found guilty and sentenced to prison). Therefore, prison populations might quite likely be void of a true representative sample of mentally retarded persons, and initial court proceedings might also be unrealistically free from retardation cases since the identification process is highly dependent upon the judge's sensitivity—but this is conjecture, since actual data are apparently unavailable.

The state of affairs is that little research has been done on the types of crimes with which mentally retarded offenders become involved. This is, indeed, a fertile area for more research; moreover, further research will be necessary before any reasonable rationale can be constructed for making assumptions about nosology.

CHAPTER FIVE

# THE MENTAL RETARDATION/ CRIMINALITY HYPOTHESIS

THE PRECEDING DISCUSSION on the kinds of crimes with which mentally retarded persons become involved provide the background for discussion of an often held hypothesis, namely that mental retardation and criminality are integrally related. That is, it is widely speculated upon and firmly believed by many that there is a significant positive relationship between mental retardation and criminality. More specifically, a superficial logic supports that mentally retarded persons, because of their intellectual deficit, are more apt to commit crimes than non-mentally retarded persons. It should be noted that care has been taken to use the term "hypothesis." The unfortunate fact is that the term "hypothesis" (which connotes a willingness to subject the hypothesis to test) has been ignored by many lay and professional persons alike. Consequently, the issue, which is in need of testing, has been misrepresented as being "fact."

One approach to testing this hypothesis would be to obtain the percentage of prisoners who are in the mentally retarded range of intellectual functioning. Obviously this approach has many methodological weaknesses, such as the lack of available test data and standardized conditions for obtaining intelligence measures, etc. Nonetheless, two studies seem to have valuable illustrative qualities.

Brown and Courtless (1968) used a questionnaire method to study a large sample of penal institutions, and they conducted case studies (e.g. follow-ups) on a sizable number of prisoners. The mean intelligence quotient (IQ) in the responding institutions was 93.2 (using the Wechsler Adult Intelligence Scale); 9.5 percent of the prisoners had an IQ below 70 and 1.6 percent had an IQ below 55. It is interesting to note that there were geographical differences; in the southern states 24.3 percent of the prisoners had an IQ below 70, whereas in the western-mountain states only 2.6 percent of the prisoners had an IQ below 70. Relevant to reliability, fifty inmates with an IQ below 70 were retested (with the Wechsler Adult Intelligence Scale); of the original fifty who had been deemed mentally retarded, the retesting yielded IQ scores below 70 for only 75 percent, with another 9 percent being classified as borderline.

Brown, Courtless, and Silber (1970) used the Wechsler Adult Intelligence Scale (W.A.I.S.) and the Thematic Apperception Test (T.A.T.) to study fantasy aggression in mentally retarded offenders. The retarded offenders did not manifest more aggressiveness; in fact, the data tended to contradict the inferred hypothesis that there was a positive correlation between retardation and aggressiveness in the mentally retarded offender sample. The investigators comment: ". . . that the retarded offender who commits a serious crime—usually a crime against a person—experiences no more, and perhaps less, aggressive motivation than his non-retarded brother. However, he may lack the inner resources to inhibit expression of such impulses when they do occur. That is, he may be unable to grasp the significance of his actions (on others or on himself)." (Brown, Courtless, and Silber, 1970.)

Relatedly, they note that the subcultures toward which society tends to push mentally retarded persons may contribute factors to the crimes, e.g. attitudes toward weapons. Regarding reliability, it is interesting that fifty-six mentally retarded offenders with an IQ below 70 (on the Wechsler Adult Intelligence Scale) were retested, and only thirty-six of them (approximately 64%) scored below a 70 IQ on the second administration. As cited in the previous discussion on diagnostic procedures (see Chapter Three), it is obvious that the test/retest data from both the Brown and Courtless (1968) and the Brown, Courtless, and Silber (1970) studies point toward poor reliability for the intelligence measures that have apparently contributed to the judicial processes and sentencing plans for mentally retarded offenders; additional comments will be made on this issue in the diagnostic section.

Levy (1953), in what is now a somewhat antiquated study, investigated the role of mental retardation in the causation of criminal behavior. He points out that many studies seem to maintain "that mental deficiency forms one of the prime sources of crime" (p. 455), but that these studies, at the time of his writing, were being recognized as sources contaminated by statistical artifacts, i.e. the results of these studies were based on faulty research designs. (Ironically, one of the major criticisms of the Levy study, as will be noted shortly, is that he tends to derive results from a research design that is inadequate for the magnitude of his conclusions—specifically, he over-generalizes his findings.) His belief is that the introduction of the genetic-dynamic concept in psychology fostered a more appropriate attitude: ". . . that there is no direct cause-and-effect relationship between any easily discernible physical and mental defect and criminality, and that criminal behavior is produced by a multiplicity of causes." Using a battery of psychological tests and interviewing methods, Levy (1953) studied new admissions to a state penitentiary. He found only 1 percent of the male population of the penitentiary could be considered "definitely feebleminded," and noted that was in accord with the incidence of mental deficiency among the general United States' population. Although numerous secondary results were obtained, he concludes: "Therefore, it is justifiable to assume, on the basis of this study, that mental deficiency *per se* does not appear to have any influence in the causation of criminal behavior since approximately the same percentage of mentally deficients which exist in the general population has been found in the population of this state penitentiary."

As mentioned earlier, while the research design is vulnerable to methodological criticisms and thus his "conclusion" may be an over-generalization of the data, it does provide an example of the doubtful relationship between mental retardation and criminality. Levy's (1953) own explanation of criminality is: "This study confirms the fact that criminality represents a bio-psycho-socio-phenomenon, and that a multiplicity of factors are at work in the causation of criminal behavior of which mental deficiency is one, and of importance only in combination with others, and that psychological, biological, and cultural factors are equally important in this connection."

Again, from the methodological point of view, it seems highly doubtful that this study confirms all that Levy purports that it does, but the interpretation does seem compatible with logical derivations from research *en masse.*

A more thorough and more contemporary (albeit still more than a decade old) review of the research relevant to the possible relationship between mental retardation and criminality has been provided by Smith (1962). He provides a review of studies dating from the early nineteenth century to the early nineteen-sixties and notes that research leaves one with "most uncertainty, disagreement, and confusion." His scholarly review leads him to six conclusions:

1. "It appears that the emphasis of the early 1900's on intellectual subnormality as a cause of crime was over-exaggerated and misleading.
2. "These most intellectually subnormal (dependent care or custodial) are least involved in delinquent and criminalistic actions. They are not seen as responsible for their behavior, and require almost total care and supervision.
3. "The trainable child (IQ 30-50) is known to require a great deal of supervision. This class of retardate is known to have little potential for economic or social independence. When their behavioral patterns do violate legal statutes, such cases are rarely considered delinquent or criminalistic, but rather the result of or lack of insight, a misunderstanding or lack of supervision.
4. "Most studies indicate that the educable mentally retarded person is represented by a higher delinquency and criminal rate than would be expected by their general prevalence in society. Here the problem is complicated by school failure and retention, early school drop outs, socio-economic status, difficulty in finding and retaining employment, inadequate societal planning for post-school life, etc. The borderline intellectual ability of the retardate is not seen necessarily implying non-conforming or norm violating behavior. How-

ever, the involved lack of insight or comprehension in such a technical, complex, and rapidly changing society creates situations which seem to penalize this segment of our society.

5. "The general study of the retardate convicted of criminal action shows a history of inadequate or broken homes, little if any supervision, poor school provisions, alcoholism, more impulsive crimes, and little ability to provide for one's economic needs successfully.
6. "There appears to be a need for society to be concerned with *life* rather than just *school* planning for the mentally retarded individual. The changing times seem to make them less able to compete on the labor market. Also, the retardate seems to need a more continued supervision of his post-school life. Most realistic school programming, as well as *more* sheltered work situations, *more* vocational rehabilitation, and *more* social work services seem necessitated. (Smith, 1962.)"

Of special relevance to hypothesis testing, strong consideration should be given to points 4 and 5 in Smith's series. In other words, although the other four points also add support for negating the belief that there is a significant positive relationship between mental retardation and criminality, points 4 and 5 provide a list of critical variables that could, and often do, overpower persons regardless of intelligence. These are variables that would be especially devastating to the mentally retarded person. Thus the mentally retarded person, for whom the intervening life-variables cited in points 4 and 5 led to his becoming a convicted criminal, would, in fact, be representing only a pseudo-correlation between mental retardation and criminality.

The foregoing evidence seems to provide ample support for the belief that, to use research terminology, the null hypothesis would be accepted; that is: *There is no significant positive relationship between mental retardation and criminality, i.e. mentally retarded persons are no more apt, because of their "below normal" intelligence, to become involved in criminality than non-mentally retarded persons.* In keeping, however, with the tenets of behavioral science, it is imperative to acknowledge that while the existing data appear to support the null hypothesis, i.e. that there is no significant positive relationship between mental retardation and criminality, this is a critical topic and one that deserves more research documentation before any "conclusive" position can be taken on the hypothesis.

CHAPTER SIX

# THE COMMON LAW, STATUTORY, AND CONSTITUTIONAL RIGHTS OF THE MENTALLY RETARDED

THE FOREMOST GOVERNMENTAL document is, without question, the United States Constitution. Its contents are designed to assure equal rights to all, regardless of any idiosyncratic characteristics. This chapter will examine whether, in point of fact, the common law, statutory, and constitutional rights of the mentally retarded are upheld in legal processes (note that statutory and constitutional rights could be at both the state and federal levels).

It is acknowledged from the onset that the number of rights presumably accorded to all persons is countless (that is, when legal formalized statements are translated into everyday life/actions). This chapter, therefore, will not delineate an exhaustive list, but will explore some of the specific rights that seem most pertinent to the mentally retarded. The present era exhibits a real flurry of legal proceedings relevant to rights in general and to the rights of the mentally retarded and the mentally ill in specific. It would, thus, be virtually impossible to present an up-to-date account of court decisions. Instead, the strategy will be to: (1) cite a few select cases that illustrate the kinds of court actions that are occurring relevant to rights of the mentally retarded; and (2) provide several references that are compendium in nature and/or references that summarize court cases recently decided or in process at the time of this writing.

Further, it should be noted that this chapter will not deal with remedies. Rather, a major objective of Chapter Ten will be to use the materials in this and other chapters as a foundation for presenting methods for specifying, facilitating, and guaranteeing rights for the mentally retarded.

## RIGHTS CRITICAL TO THE MENTALLY RETARDED

It goes without saying that any legal human right is important to each mentally retarded person. The heading of this section and the contents herein are directed at delineating those rights that are of *particular* importance to the mentally retarded person; in other words, it is a matter of identifying those rights that must be maintained because of the mentally retarded condition.

An appropriate introduction to this topic seems to be the comprehensive statement titled "Declaration on the Rights of Mentally Retarded Persons" that was adopted as a resolution by the United Nations (1971). Following a statement of the rationale for the United Nations' involvement with this issue, seven rights were set forth:

1. "The mentally retarded person has, to the maximum degree of feasibility, the same rights as other human beings.
2. "The mentally retarded person has a right to proper medical care and physical therapy and to such education, training, rehabilitation and guidance as will enable him to develop his ability and maximum potential.
3. "The mentally retarded person has a right to economic security and to a decent standard of living. He has a right to perform productive work, or to engage in any other meaningful occupation to the fullest possible extent of his capabilities.
4. "Whenever possible, the mentally retarded person should live with his own family or with foster parents and participate in different forms of community life. The family with which he lives should receive assistance. If care in an institution becomes necessary, it should be provided in surroundings and other circumstances as close as possible to those of normal life.
5. "The mentally retarded person has a right to a qualified guardian when this is required to protect his personal well-being and interests.
6. "The mentally retarded person has a right to protection from exploitation, abuse and degrading treatment. If prosecuted for any offense, he shall have a right to due process of law

with full recognition being given to his degree of mental responsibility.

7. "Whenever mentally retarded persons are unable, because of the severity of their handicap, to exercise all their rights in a meaningful way or it should become necessary to restrict or deny some or all of these rights, the procedure used for that restriction or denial of rights must contain proper legal safeguards against every form of abuse. This procedure must be based on an evaluation of the social capability of the mentally retarded person by qualified experts and must be subject to periodic review and to the right of appeal to higher authorities."

The United Nations charged that this Resolution ". . . calls for national and international action to ensure that it will be used as a common basis and frame of reference for the protection of these rights" (United Nations, 1971).

This document from such a prestigious source gave impetus to already mushrooming concern and actions on behalf of the mentally retarded from lay-community and professional mental/public health organizations. The result has been a myriad of legal proceedings.

To turn directly to the principal objective of this section, the delineation of those rights that must be maintained because of the mentally retarded condition, Ogg (1973) emphasizes that mentally retarded persons in the community certainly have a right to the civil rights afforded to all citizens, along with the right to education and the right to the least restrictive alternative. This posture moves naturally enough toward the issues of the right to training for a job, the right to avoid compulsory sterilization, and the right to guardianship; and in the case of mentally retarded persons needing institutionalization, Ogg points toward the rights for treatment, freedom from involuntary servitude, protection from abuse, and due process. These rights are compatible with those elucidated by the Mental Health Law Project (1973), which divided the "basic rights of the mentally handicapped" into the following three areas: (1) the right to treatment; (2) the right to compensation for institution-maintaining labor; and (3) the right to education. Furthermore, in a report on current court cases, Friedman (1973) "featured" the right to treatment, and, in addition, reviewed cases dealing with the right to public education, the right to fair classification, the right to compensation for institution maintaining labor, and legal issues related to custody and commitment laws. These same categories of rights seem to emerge in two compendia of litigation: the President's Committee on Mental Retardation (1973) established a Legal Rights Work Group to compile a compendium of class action law suits related to the legal rights of the mentally retarded, and the Council for Exceptional Children (Abeson, 1973) initiated what is termed "a continuing summary" of litigation relevant to the education of handicapped children. One of the most comprehensive compilations is a three volume series titled *Legal Rights of the Mentally Handicapped* (Ennis and Friedman, 1973a, 1973b, 1973c).

Reference to the sources cited in the preceding paragraph would, obviously, lead to a more informed stance on specific aspects of the various rights critical to mental retardation. Such a review leads to the conclusion that the following areas particularly merit consideration: civil liberties in general, the right to guardianship, the right to protective services, the right to treatment (with the latter being defined generically enough to encompass the right to education), and the rights to marry and have children. This grouping will also allow for considering numerous issues, many of which touch on or are related to the other rights previously identified.

## CIVIL LIBERTIES IN GENERAL

The most basic issue is that when a person is judged to be mentally retarded (or mentally ill) to the degree that he cannot handle his own affairs (or may be a jeopardy to others), he may be placed under the jurisdiction of the court. Most commonly this means placement in an institution, which in turn means that the person's individual rights are transferred to a guardian, such as the superintendent of the state institution in which he is placed ("guardianship" will be considered in detail later in this chapter).

For a cross-cultural comparative perspective, Bray (1971) has provided an analysis of the legal rights of the mentally retarded, with special reference to their civil liberties, in Australia. As might be expected, there are many commonalities between common law in Australia and the United States. With the common law of England providing a historical backdrop, he notes what is probably one of the most fundamental factors:

> First of all let me say that the phrase "mentally retarded person" is unknown to the common law. Broadly speaking, the common law only knows two classes for this purpose—the sane and the insane, although the test of insanity is not necessarily the same in all contexts. The 1964 amendment to the South Australian Mental Health Act refers to persons who are mentally ill or intellectually retarded. This replaces the term "mental defective" as that term replaced the word "lunatic," another illustration of the inveterate tendency of the human mind to imagine that you can change realities by changing names, when all you do is to spoil the language by sending the unpleasant association of the old words to gather round the new.

The Australian definitions were, of course, presented in Chapter Two, and the important point to underscore within this quote is that: ". . . the phrase 'mentally retarded' persons is unknown to the common law." In this connection, Bray points out: "There is no general statute dealing with the rights, obligations, liabilities or incapacities of mentally afflicted persons not officially declared to be such." Thus the point is introduced that, to gain unique rights, the mentally retarded person must go through the legal procedures for being "declared." With this as a frame of reference, Bray (1971) discusses: ". . . the effect of unsoundness of mind on the capacity to make dispositions of property, including wills, to enter into contracts generally, on marriage and divorce, on the power legally to consent to sexual intercourse, the liability of civil wrongs, criminal liability, the capacity to bring and defend civil actions and finally, on a few miscellaneous matters."

Although he deals with a great number of elements within the law that would apply to declared and undeclared mentally retarded persons or "persons of unsound mind," it will suffice to highlight the following:

> A person who lacks the capacity to understand the nature of the transaction in question cannot dispose of his property.
>
> The Real Property Act (sec. 244-245) provides that the court may appoint a guardian of any idiot or lunatic and such guardian can give such consents and do such acts with regard to land registered under the Act as the idiot or lunatic himself might have done if free from incapacity.
>
> Under the present law a marriage is void if either party is mentally incapable of understanding the nature of the marital contract. . . .
>
> Any husband or wife can petition for divorce on the ground that the other spouse is, at the date of the petition, of unsound mind and unlikely to recover and has been confined in one or more institutions for the mentally afflicted for periods aggregating not less than five years since the marriage and within the six years immediately preceding the petition. . . .
>
> . . . it is provided that any person who unlawfully and carnally knows or attempts to have unlawful carnal knowledge of any female idiot or imbecile woman or girl under circumstances which do not amount to rape, but which prove that the offender knew at the time of the commission of the offense that the woman or girl was an idiot or imbecile shall be guilty of a misdemeanor and liable to imprisonment for any term not exceeding seven years.
>
> An action to which a mentally defective person is party cannot be compromised without the leave of the court, nor can any money which he may receive as the result of any judgment or compromise be paid out to him or dealt with without the leave of the court.
>
> A person of unsound mind is not qualified to vote for either house of either the State or Federal Parliament. . . .
>
> . . . the Commissioner of Police or the Registrar may suspend the driving license of any person whom he suspects to be suffering from any disease, mental or physical, which impairs his ability to drive a motor vehicle.
>
> . . . no person whose estate is administered by the Public Trustee, or of whose estate a committee has been appointed under the Act, shall be capable without the leave of the court of making any conveyance, transfer, lease or mortgage or other disposition of any contract, except for necessaries.

What should be clearly evident is that the Australian laws, while presumably developed to safeguard the rights of the citizens, may actually be grossly restricting certain classes of the citizens, such as the mentally retarded, at least in some instances. And there is definitely room for poor reliability to appear. For example, note that in the removal of a driving license, the statute allows the governmental authority to do so if he "suspects" that there is a condition that impairs driving ability; one might wonder how much agreement there would be between several Commissioners of Police if they acted upon a uniform set of data about a mentally retarded person's ability to drive. For example, would driving ability be reliably evaluated in cases involving a mentally retarded person from a high socio-economic class as compared to a person from a low socio-economic class?

In this age of efforts to avoid sex discrimination, the statute protecting female mentally retarded persons from sexual activities introduces two interesting considerations. First, it precludes mentally retarded females expressing their sexuality; Bray (1971) comments: ". . . many feeble minded women are capable of understanding broadly the nature of the act of sexual intercourse, and even of enjoying it and seeking it. . . ." But further, and in the interest of avoiding discrimination because of the sex of the person, it is intriguing to note that Bray (1971) states: "The converse case of a woman having sexual intercourse with a mentally defective man is not specifically dealt with by legislation. However, if such a man is incapable of consent by reason of his mental condition, it may be that a woman could commit an indecent assault upon him in the course of sexual intercourse or the preliminaries thereto." Sometimes the law works in wondrous ways!

As mentioned, there are commonalities between the laws of Australia and the United States. Therefore, to avoid repetition of many of the same points covered in the writings of Bray (1971), it should be noted that Haggerty, Kane, and Udall (1972) describe many of the same kinds of violations of civil and criminal rights for mentally retarded persons in the United States. To cite but a few instances, they comment on the lack of an adversary system when institutionalization is being considered and state: "In the area of rights that stem from living in a community, rights enjoyed by all 'normal' citizens, the retarded person is almost always deprived of his right to enter into a contract (to marry or even to buy a secondhand car); to be licensed (for such diverse activities as driving a car or being a barber); and to vote, that most American right."

They also point out the deprivation of the right to have children, e.g. forced sterilization, the right to heterosexual contact (a practice forbidden in many institutions), the right to education (and frequently to treatment and/or rehabilitation), and the right to buy insurance. Finally, ". . . in the most extreme cases, the retarded person may be deprived of the right to life itself." Regarding criminal rights, Haggerty, Kane, and Udall believe that the failure to distinguish the mentally retarded person from others, such as to distinguish them from the mentally ill, may lead to a loss of rights in criminal court proceedings. They purport that this is particularly true when information is garnered from the mentally retarded person accused of a crime:

> Where the mentally retarded defendant is in fact innocent and the case does go to trial, he or she is again disadvantaged by the characteristics of the deficiency. The retarded person is more likely to confess than is the normal person. According to the President's Panel on Mental Retardation, "The retarded are particularly vulnerable to an atmosphere of threats and coercion, as well as to one of friendliness designed to induce confidence and cooperation . . . if a confession will please, it may be gladly given." Conversely, the retarded person is less likely to be able to withstand hard cross-examination or direct questioning by an aggressive prosecutor. To the great majority of jurors, not to mention judges, his behavior will not square with their concept of innocence.

Haggerty, Kane, and Udall point out that, because of the intellectual deficit, "The *Miranda* decision has had little effect on the rights of the retarded," and that: "While the process of arrest, interrogation and trial is traumatic for a normal individual, it is far more frightening to a retarded person and far more destructive of his emotional and nervous system." There seems no room to question, in view of the comments by Bray (1971) and by Haggerty, Kane, and Udall (1972), that the rights of the mentally retarded are, in fact, withheld to a degree not appropriated to "normal" citizens.

Intrinsic to this is the matter of the commitment, whether the person voluntarily seeks it or whether it is involuntarily imposed upon him. Robitscher (1972a) states unequivocally that "involuntary mental hospitalization is a deprivation of liberty"; and this ties into his belief that there is a "right to treatment" (which will be discussed subsequently in detail). Robitscher justifies the right to treatment: "The benefit that accrues to patients who get adequate psychiatric treatment enables them to regain their liberty at the earliest possible time and so gives legal legitimacy to the hospitalization." Although state statutes differ, there seems to be an ample number of reasons, both legal and therapeutic, for endorsing voluntary commitment; moreover, strategies are available to increase the frequency of voluntary versus involuntary commitments (Schwartz and Dumpman, 1972).

The foregoing introduces four primary areas of rights: the right to guardianship, the right to protective services, the right to treatment, and the right to marry and have children.

## THE RIGHT TO GUARDIANSHIP

In view of their presumed limited intellectual capacity, *some* mentally retarded persons could logically benefit from guardianship. The assumption is, of course, that the appointed guardian is, in fact, someone who has the best interest of the mentally retarded person as an objective. The rationale is: "Guardianship proceedings are, essentially, a methodology for taking over the management of business affairs for someone who cannot look after these things for himself and, in the case of guardianship of the person, for someone who cannot make responsible decisions for his own care." (Lehman, 1961.)

Ober (1963) indicated that there are several kinds of guardians that are recognized legally: "The natural guardian is the lawful parent of a child. A legal guardian is one appointed by the court for either a child or an adult. A testamentary guardian is anyone designated guardian by the last will and testament of the child's parents. Guardian *ad litem* is one appointed by the court for a particular act and is usually temporary and specific in nature."

Another form of guardianship is the so-called "public guardian," which is a public official empowered by the court to act as a legal guardian. Ober (1963) states that: ". . . guardianship is the ultimate in protective services. Ultimate because it denies to the individual, by legal action, all rights for self-determination and vests those rights in another individual."

Of special relevance to the issue of reliability, which is the central theme of this book, Ober (1953) notes that: ". . . no standard criteria exist for selecting guardians. . . . The court will usually appoint anyone as guardian . . . who is willing to be named guardian and who is not obviously unfit to serve."

Further comments by Ober and other legal sources (e.g. Kay, Farnham, Karren, Knakal, and Diamond, 1972) reveal that there is certainly no consistent system for assuring that the fulfillment of the objective, i.e. selecting a guardian who will optimally safeguard the rights of the client, will attain respectable validity or reliability. Szasz and Alexander (1972) question that the existing guardianship system actually protects the alleged incompetent.

An improvement in the guardianship system, such as might be applicable to the mentally retarded, may be possible. Ober (1963) offers the following nine guidelines:

1. "That the process of determination of need of guardianship remain a judicial function.
2. "That guardianship be reserved to all those adult mentally retarded in whom the reduction of social competency is so marked that persistent social dependency shall have been demonstrated or anticipated.
3. "That the disciplines of medicine, psychology and social work present evidence to the adjudicating court that persistent social dependency has been demonstrated or is to be anticipated.
4. "That guardianship for the adult mentally retarded be sought by parents so that this legal right to direct the incompetent's affairs is established and vested in the person of the parent's choice.
5. "That a 'public guardianship program' be established and

be administered by a state agency having acceptable procedures for accountability.

6. "That interested and responsible parents, relatives and friends of the one requiring guardianship be considered first for the office of guardian.
7. "That institutionalized adult retardates as they approach their majority be considered in regard to the need for guardianship and legal guardians be appointed for those who are found to qualify.
8. "That guardianship of person and property be separated if the interest of the retarded is thus best served.
9. "That the guardian of the person be made accountable for the discharge of his responsibility for the care and management of his ward and the guardian of property—for the care and management of his property."

While these are succinct and seemingly logical recommendations that could presumably improve the guardianship system for the mentally retarded, it can almost go without saying that political, social, and bureaucratic factors will hamper actual implementation. Szasz and Alexander (1972) offer a three-point plan:

> Briefly, it was suggested that 1) whenever possible, persons incapable of managing their property (for whatever reason) be encouraged to seek surrogate managers voluntarily; 2) the "legitimate" interests of certain persons in the property of others (especially within the family) be formally recognized and protected by law; and, 3) the proceeding for involuntary intervention in property management be removed from the sphere of psychiatry and be placed squarely into that of the law.

The authors definitely question the reliability of the guardianship system, since it is likely that undue emphasis may be placed on the allegedly incompetent person needing someone to manage his affairs for his own best interest, and they caustically assert that such ". . . may be true not only for persons deemed to be incompetent, but for virtually everyone!" Apparently, this remark suggests that at some point in time there are always others who could claim to be more knowledgeable about and capable of managing another person's affairs than the person himself—competent or incompetent.

While guardianship is, in many ways, the ultimate in protective services, another protective service, which is indeed a "right" is reflected in the following statements regarding the right to psychiatric representation; that is, the mentally retarded person in a legal system has the following rights:

> To obtain for himself the expert whom he trusts most.
> To challenge the competency of the opposition expert.
> To have the court hear both sides.
> To have the element of intent or *mens rea,* when an essential part of a crime, proved by the prosecution.
> To have a choice of pleading insanity or not as his own best interest indicates.
> To be free from enforced psychiatric examination before arraignment, when no crime is charged.
> To have conflicting opinions made a matter of public record, so that they can be considered by a superior court of appeal and brought to the attention of the public through the press.
> To have a conviction based on the opinion of the jury.
> To have the advantage of a presumption of innocence.
> To prevent the deification of a single point of view. (Robitscher, 1966.)

Because of the high esteem attributed to our legal system, a first glance at these rights might lead to a response of: "How naive can you be? Of course those rights are upheld!" Unfortunately, such is not the case.

In the quest for reliability relevant to the presence of mental retardation, there is evidence that judges and court workers lack understanding of and consistent means for dealing with mental retardation (Kay, Farnham, Karren, Knakal, and Diamond, 1972). Brown and Courtless (1968) found that few mentally retarded prisoners had benefit of legal counsel and expert testimony at any time during their legal processing. Further, in a study by Haggerty, Kane, and Udall (1972), based on information for the Law and Ethics Work Group sponsored by the President's Committee on Mental Retardation, it was revealed that the "experts" involved in the aforementioned studies were surprised and shocked at the way in which mentally retarded persons were processed in the American system of criminal justice. For example, one informant stated ". . . that he thought a reasonable estimate of those lawyers who have some familiarity with the problems of the mentally retarded to be 'perhaps one-half of one percent.' " Many of these issues are also tied into Chapter Eight on the administrative and judicial handling of the mentally retarded, but it merits underscoring at this point that clearly delineated legal rights, which are interrelated with protective services, are often negated with mentally retarded persons (often perhaps because of a lack of understanding of mental retardation).

## THE RIGHT TO PROTECTIVE SERVICES

Protective services are predicated on the assumption that mentally retarded persons, because of their intellectual deficit, are entitled to professional services that will improve and make their existence more comfortable. This rationale is particularly applicable to those who have had their rights removed via placement in a state institution.

There are several dimensions to the protective services composite. Allen (1968), using an analysis of the laws for seven states as a basis, delineated the following eight principles that must be maintained to have effective protective services:

> *First, protective services do not protect when legal proceedings become routinized and pro forma and when decision-makers lose sight of both the nature of the services available and the needs of the people to be served.*
>
> *Second, protective services do not protect when there is a lack of adequate staff and physical facilities.*
>
> *Third, protective services do not protect when important decision-makers are ignorant of them or of their appropriate use.*
>
> *Fourth, protective services do not protect when they impose coercive sanctions unnecessarily, or for longer periods than necessary, or when more appropriate noncoercive measures are available.*
>
> *Fifth, protective services do not protect when the legal provisions under which they may be rendered are phrased in terms which, because of their ambiguity or inappropriateness, make it difficult to identify the categories of persons eligible to receive them.*
>
> *Sixth, protective services do not protect when custodial care, because of its ease of application, becomes the treatment of choice over other*

*protective services more appropriate to the needs of the retardate.*

*Seventh, protective services do not protect when they are rendered by a multiplicity of agencies with ambiguously defined and often overlapping jurisdiction.*

*Eighth, and finally (for the present writing), protective services do not protect when they do not respect the dignity and worth of the individual.*

The importance of citing each of these guidelines verbatim is two-fold. First, they demonstrate the interconnections between protective services and all of the other chapters and sections in this book, such as the topics of diagnostics, classifications, etc., in that these other areas are of crucial significance to the attainment of effective protective services. And second, and perhaps foremost, these guidelines are integrally dependent upon the reliability concept in order to be fulfilled; i.e. each guideline contains a point that must be avoided (or stated conversely, that must be achieved) in order for protective services to truly protect. Such an honorable consummation cannot occur without these protective functions being conducted in a highly reliable fashion.

## THE RIGHT TO TREATMENT

The discussion thus far in this chapter has dealt, for the most part, with the rights of the retarded in general, although references to specific rights have also been made. It would appear that the major practical right for the mentally retarded is: the right to treatment (as mentioned previously, the right to treatment will be defined generically enough to encompass the right to education).

The right to treatment has reached prominence, perhaps even notoriety, because of a recent court decision in the State of Alabama (*Wyatt v. Stickney,* 325, *Federal Supplement,* 781-786, 1971); it should be noted that appeal has shifted the identifying names to *Wyatt v. Aderholt.* Robitscher (1972a), in an analysis of the "Alabama Case," points out that the court mandated that the purpose of involuntary hospitalization was *treatment* and was not custodial care or punishment, and that the judge: ". . . specified the three fundamental conditions that his court would examine to ascertain if adequate and effective treatment was available. These were: 1) a humane psychological and physical environment; 2) qualified staff in number sufficient to administer adequate treatment; and 3) individualized treatment plans." It is interesting that the court specified environmental details and entered into setting standards for treatment; for example, the court prescribed acceptable levels of professional training and acceptable ratios between patients and professional mental health workers in the institutions.

Because of the furor created in lay, legal, and professional mental health circles by this judicial ruling, it might be easy to lose sight of the real issue: the right to treatment concept. "The concept has been often misunderstood because the right to treatment is a shorthand expression for much more than a statement about health care delivery; it means the right of involuntarily hospitalized mental patients to receive adequate therapy as an exchange for their being deprived of their liberty." (Robitscher, 1972a.)

At the risk of redundancy, the latter part of the preceding quote deserves restatement for emphasis: ". . . the right of involuntarily hospitalized mental patients to receive adequate therapy as an exchange for their being deprived of their liberty." The emphasis is on "adequate therapy" in exchange for one's "liberty" or "rights." Additional information on the right to treatment concept can be gained from Friedman (1973), the Mental Health Law Project (1973), and Morris (1970).

To some authorities, the withholding of certain opportunities falls into the classification of class discrimination. Knudson (1969) states: "It is submitted that to draw class lines so as to permit the bright student, as well as the average student, to receive free education while denying free care and treatment to the retardate whose condition is such that he requires constant supervision in a public institution is an improper narrowing of the classification where the legislative purpose is to perform a public service."

Knudson (1969) also addresses himself to the question of who should pay for services for the mentally retarded, and his answer is straightforward:

> The test should be limited to one question: Is the person a danger or potential danger to the community? If the answer is in the affirmative, his confinement is for the purpose of protecting the society; thus, its members should bear the cost of protecting themselves. Theoretically at least, the only difference between a criminal commitment and a civil one based on danger to the public, is that one has already committed a crime while the other merely poses a future threat.

These statements relate nicely to the reliability concept. If citizens have a right to "treatment" services, which, according to a generic definition, would encompass public education, then there must be consistency, i.e. reliability, in the implementing and funding of opportunities regardless of class lines.

Within this discussion of the right to treatment for the mentally retarded, the most overriding connotation is probably the right to medical and/or psychotherapeutic treatment, i.e. forms of professional intervention that will facilitate the mentally retarded person's adjustment to his life-style and that will potentially maximize his chances for eliminating the handicapping effects of below average intellect. The term "habilitation" has, however, become a much-endorsed posture within the issue of the right to treatment. Based on the case of *Wyatt v. Stickney,* Murdock (1972) presents the following definition: " 'Habilitation'—the process by which the staff of the institution assists the resident to acquire and maintain those life skills which enable him to cope more effectively with the demands of his own person and of his environment and to raise the level of his physical, mental, and social efficiency. Habilitation includes but is not limited to programs of formal structured education and treatment." The important distinction between treatment being defined in the traditional "therapeutic" model and the more contemporary "habilitation" model is that the latter gives greater credence to adaptation relevant to the individual and his particular subculture and to developmental potential. Habilitation is also quite compatible with the ultimate goal for helping mentally retarded persons: Normalization. *Normalization,* as a theoretical concept with practical implications, will be dealt with in Chapter Ten.

It is important to point out that the right to treatment can also be reworded to be the "right to education." Starting perhaps with the now famous *Brown v. Board of Education* (347, *Federal Supplement,* 483-493, 1954), the Supreme Court decision that voided segregation of school children on the basis of race, there have been several subsequent decisions that have had direct implications for the education of mentally retarded persons. For example, the decision in *Hobson v. Hansen* (269, *Federal Supplement,* 401-518, 1967) questioned the "tracking system" and the use of standardized psychological and educational tests (many of which were presumably culturally biased) within the District of Columbia's public school system, with the decision supporting that Negro and poor children (regardless of race) had the right to an opportunity for education equal to more affluent public school children. In the case of the *Pennsylvania Association of Retarded Children v. the Commonwealth of Pennsylvania* (334, *Federal Supplement,* 1257-1269, 1971), it was concluded that mentally retarded children were entitled to free public education and training. Lippman and Goldberg (1973) provide a detailed analysis of the "Pennsylvania Case" and discuss its implications for exceptional children. Finally, in the case of *Mills et al. v. the District of Columbia Board of Education* (348, *Federal Supplement,* 866-883, 1972), a decision was rendered, based on both constitutional rights and a statutory basis, that educational provisions had to be made for those students placed in the categories of special education, behavioral problems, mental retardation, and emotional disturbance. Abeson (1973) summarizes many other cases relevant to the rights to education and treatment. Although it would appear that progressive legal actions are being taken to establish the right of the mentally retarded person to educational opportunities equal to those provided to non-mentally retarded persons, it is obvious that probably few public school systems in the country actually attain such equality and thus do not consistently, i.e. do not reliably, fulfill the right. Lippman and Goldberg (1973) provide valuable information as to the implications of and implementation methods for the right to education in public school systems.

In his essay on the civil rights of the mentally retarded, Murdock (1972) focuses on three critical issues: guardianship, institutionalization, and education. The most cogent point for this discussion is that he identifies education as a "fundamental interest" of our society, noting: "There is no question that the equal protection clause applies to eligibility for a public educational program." Murdock's concluding posture is one of maintaining that mentally retarded persons cannot be excepted from this equal protection right:

> Of the three topics considered in this article, guardianship, institutionalization, and education, the prospects for the retarded appear the brightest in the area of education. Not only is there a federal constitutional basis for arguing that the retarded are entitled to a public education, but also the same result is mandated by many of the state constitutions, which require the establishment of a public educational system that is open to all. Moreover, the requirement of upgrading the quality of habilitation in state institutions, and the concomitant cost spiral resulting therefrom, will create tremendous pressures to provide services to the retarded outside the traditional, huge warehouse-type institution. Finally, the number of special educational programs and the awareness of the long-run financial benefits flowing from such programs has been increasing. (Murdock, 1972.)

There is still much controversy surrounding the broad issue of the right to treatment, and as much or more controversy is directed at the more circumspect issue of the right to education for the mentally retarded. It appears, however, that rapid clarification is developing, and that the trend appears to be distinctly in favor of specifying a right to education for the mentally retarded. As yet, the issue is unreliably handled, but it seems logical to predict that in the near future more careful specification will carry with it the much needed reliability.

Since the rationale for the right to treatment is controversial, to say the least, a clear conceptualization is necessary. Bazelon (1969) states:

> The rationale for the right to treatment is clear. If society confines a man for the benevolent purpose of helping him—"for his own good," in the standard phrase—then its right to so withhold his freedom depends entirely upon whether help is in fact provided. It may be that the person is not treatable or that the treatment effort is too costly in light of the chances of success. If this is the view of the professional, it should be spread clearly upon the record so that we do not delude

> ourselves by calling these unfortunates "patients." But whatever care is simply custodial, we must be certain beyond a reasonable doubt—and I import this legal phrase deliberately—that the individual truly could not hope to care for himself. And when the rationale for institutionalization is not that the person would be dangerous to himself, but that he would be dangerous to others, we must be even more careful. Whatever justification we may find in theories of retribution or general deterrence for confining a convicted criminal, the case is quite different when the individual has committed no crime. Confinement in this situation is, to employ an emotive but accurate term, preventive detention. As such, it is appropriate, if ever, only when the probability of future harmful conduct is high indeed. And when prediction is impossible, we cannot ask the individual to suffer from our uncertainty.

The main impact of this statement is, of course, philosophical. But intrinsic to it is the reoccurring theme of the need for consistency or reliability of judgment and execution of actions. As one clear example, there is emphasis placed on the need to predict the individual's future behavior and the consequences for himself and others, i.e. society. Such predictions, as will be elaborated upon in more detail later, frequently fail to attain a respectable degree of reliability—even when the most expert of professional judgments are used for the prediction.

In all fairness to the legal system and to add clarity to the right to treatment concept, it should be pointed out that while some courts may specify ratios for the patients and professional staff members or may delineate the quality of services in other ways, these guidelines or indices are, almost inevitably, somewhat arbitrary. Thus no one decision with an inherent set of criteria for what would fulfill "adequate treatment" can be taken as a prototype void of any need for refinement or change. Each case, i.e. each patient, and each context for treatment, must be given an idiosyncratic appraisal. Bazelon (1969) indicates: "The most important fact of the right to treatment is not that the hospital does something for everyone, but that it does the right thing for the right patient. Because individual patients, particularly mental patients, vary so much in their needs, considerable attention must be paid to the patient as an individual." And because of this, he adds: "Any legislative definition of adequate treatment should therefore insure not only that the hospital provides treatment in general, but also that it tailors the treatment offered to the specific treatment."

Although the right to treatment seems to be finding increasing support from judicial decisions, it is an extremely complex concept to make operational, not to mention to make practical. At the present time, it would appear that the implementation of the right to treatment concept will meet with many barriers, some of which may be attributable to the newness and the extent of acceptance being accorded to it and some of which may be attributable to the pragmatic issues, e.g. costs to radically alter the quality of treatment within state-supported facilities. But many of these barriers may also be tied into the adequacy of our legal system, as evident when Bazelon (1969) states that ". . . we simply lack the administrative machinery and legislative standards necessary. . . ." He points out that there is a negative argument against moving ahead with departures from traditional elements of our legal system, namely that it ". . . leads not to the conclusion that the right to treatment is intrinsically unwise or unenforceable, but only to the proposition that courts cannot implement the right without the aid of a legislative framework." Reliability for the implementation of the right to treatment concept is, therefore, inextricably involved with the need to evolve a more effective legislative system and to, as a resulting concomitant, evolve more efficient administrative and legal procedures.

It is evident that new approaches must be devised and implemented, and in so doing that new sources of data for consideration will have to be admitted. Two points stand out: first, treatment must be for all, regardless of any class characteristic, and second, objective measures must be devised.

Regarding treatment for all, there are many possible examples, but one of the most cogent is services for youth (versus services for adults). Because children are the responsibility of their parents, many professionals have asserted that children and youth may actually lack rights; that is, their parents control their rights (Polier, 1968). Shong (1972) has provided a review of theories of delinquency, causation, relevant statutes (e.g. liability without fault), liability of parents, and selected cases, all for the purpose of clarifying that the legal responsibility for children's delinquency does rest with the parents. The situation, then, is that youth—without question a major portion of our population in sheer numbers alone and a critical resource because of their potential to evolve into being the contributing members of our society—are to some degree neglected by the law, their rights and responsibilities abrogated to their parents. Yet Pyfer (1972) notes that: ". . . juvenile crime now accounts for as much as 24 percent of all arrests and approximately 45 percent of all serious offenses. Ninety percent of all young people have committed at least one act for which they could have been brought to juvenile court."

His review of legal actions is used to develop a rationale for juveniles' right to receive treatment on constitutional bases, to receive due process (e.g. since the United States Supreme Court has characterized due process as more than a doctrine of law and as being "fundamental to a civilized society"), and to receive equal protection. In regard to the latter, equal protection, Pyfer states: "While *parens patriae* and rehabilitation are invoked to secure divestment of the offending child from the criminal process, he remains subject to involuntary deprivation of liberty which may extend far beyond the statutory criminal punishment imposed on an adult convicted of similar conduct."

Of particular importance relevant to the right to treatment for juveniles, reference is made to the 1968 Uniform Juvenile Court Act, which promulgated:

> 1. to provide for the care, protection, and wholesome moral, mental and physical development of children . . . ;
> 2. consistent with the protection of the public interest, to remove from children committing delinquent acts the taint of criminality and the consequences of criminal behavior and to *substitute therefor a program of treatment, training, and rehabilitation;*
> 3. to achieve the foregoing purposes in a family environment whenever possible, separating the child from his parents only when necessary for his welfare or in the interest of public safety. . . . (Pyfer, 1972.)

It would seem that the right to treatment could not be more pronounced. But as with Bazelon's (1969) cautionary statements, Pyfer (1972) reacts to the Uniform Juvenile Court Act by saying: "But merely recodifying well-intentioned theory cannot camouflage the court's failure to achieve its goals. In theory, rehabilitation was to be accomplished through individualized care and treatment. In reality, the truth is simply that the younger a person is when first arrested, the more likely he is to return to prison."

As was true with so much of the foregoing material, there has to be a challenge set forth, and regarding the juveniles' right to treatment Pyfer (1972) asserts: "Until the administrative problems of providing adequate treatment are solved, clearly establishing the constitutional right to treatment remains the surest way of protecting the liberty and interest of all civil commitments. The right not to be civilly punished must be established if justice and rehabilitation are to become an integrated reality." The ultimate challenge is to establish a reliable constitutional commitment to the right to treatment, regardless of age group.

The second area noted previously that is critical to the development of new approaches to the right to treatment is the devising of objective measures. Nothing could be more relevant to the topic of reliability, because subjectivity, the antithesis of objectivity, is the bane to achieving respectability. Robitscher (1972a) has spoken against conceptualizing the right to treatment ". . . as an automatic consequence of improved patient-staff ratios or greater per patient expenditures. . . ." Instead, the right to treatment is viewed as a mandate for a changed attitude within psychiatry (note that "psychiatry" should be interpreted generically, thereby connoting all of the mental health specialties). Robitscher states:

> As difficult as the measurement of good psychiatric care may be (and it is even more difficult than the measurement of good medical care), some objective standards will have to be set by psychiatry so that patients, third party payees, state legislatures, and courts can compare hospital *A* and hospital *B*, treatment *A* and treatment *B*, psychiatrist *A* and psychiatrist *B*. The myth that all psychiatric care is equivalent to all other psychiatric care must be abandoned, and realistic methods of appraisal of care must be substituted. (Robitscher, 1972a.)

He adds that "the measurement of psychiatric effectiveness is belatedly receiving attention. . . ." Here is a mandate that, at the risk of redundancy, announces that the attainment of objective appraisals, which cannot exist without a respectably high degree of reliability, is prerequisite to the fulfillment of the right to treatment.

## THE RIGHT TO MARRY AND TO HAVE CHILDREN

Two other areas of rights deserve brief mention: the right to marry and the right to have children. Both are complex issues for mentally retarded persons, and the scope of this section does not accommodate detailed exploration of either of them, but the key concern can be specified.

Reference was made earlier to the fact that legally declared mentally retarded persons cannot, in most circumstances, enter into contracts, and marriage is, of course, a contract: "For it to come into effect, courts have held, the parties marrying must have sufficient mental competency to understand the nature of the contract that they are entering into and to understand that they are in fact getting married." (Robitscher, 1966.)

In view of the other kinds of restrictions imposed on the mentally retarded, many of which are of course *presumably* for their own welfare, the law has not been silent about mentally retarded persons marrying:

> Besides the general principles governing marriage of the mentally disabled, many states have passed laws that specifically prohibit the marriage of some people regardless of whether they have the competency to enter into a marriage contract. Two reasons are given for such statutes: the first is to prevent the creation of a marriage when one prospective partner lacks sufficient reason fully to understand the nature of the contract (i.e. rather than dealing with the individual and ascertaining whether he has competency, the fact that the individual has been placed in a special category before the law automatically brings into effect the prohibition against marriage) . . . . The second reason for statutory prohibitions of marriage is eugenic—to prevent the birth of children who may be constitutionally or environmentally handicapped. (Robitscher, 1966.)

In his treatise on the status of the mentally ill in America, Deutsch (1946) asserted that, throughout the states with relevant laws, legal statutes designed to prevent marriage between the mentally disabled have ". . . invariably proved worthless, chiefly because of the lack of adequate provision for the identification or diagnosis of the mental status of applicants for marriage licenses." Thus the failure of these laws, according to Deutsch's pinpointing of the inadequacy for identification and diagnosis, reintroduces the reliability concept. The assumption is that, given valid and reliable means for "identification and diagnosis of the mental status of applicants for marriage licenses," the statutes could have, in fact, proven to be of value for protecting mentally retarded persons from entering into contracts, e.g. a marriage contract, that were beyond their intellectual capability to understand.

Giving consideration to the right of the mentally retarded to have children (particularly those who are patients in a state facility for the mentally retarded), one could introduce a multitude of viewpoints, facts, opinions, and issues. As mentioned, such will not be the case herein. Suffice it to say that for decades legislation of various types has been enacted in the majority of the states that allow, with differing restrictions and criteria, eugenic sterilization. Ferster (1966) provides a comprehensive review of the legislation, case decisions, and statistics regarding sterilization practices. The rationale for involuntary eugenic sterilization may be summarized as follows: "Involuntary eugenic sterilization was advocated to save civilization from the imminent danger of being overrun by defective stocks who were already eating it away like internal parasites. Mental illness, mental retardation, epilepsy and criminality were all believed to be hereditary. Consequently, cure for these conditions was hopeless and prevention was the only answer. For example, it was alleged if sterilization was permitted the total number of retardates would be 'greatly reduced in one generation and might in several generations be practically rooted out of the human race.' " (Ferster, 1966.)

Although still in existence, both legally and illegally (there is evidence that sterilizations frequently are illegally performed and are unreported!), there does seem to be a decrease in the number of sterilizations:

> The legal basis for involuntary eugenic sterilization exists but the number of operations decreases each year. During the last two dec-

> ades, there has been increasing opposition to sterilization on the grounds that scientific knowledge of hereditary factors in mental disability is not sufficient to warrant its widespread use, certainly not an involuntary basis. There is also opposition to sterilization on theological, moral and social grounds. However, the objections on scientific grounds seem to have been the major cause of the drop in the number of sterilizations. (Ferster, 1966.)

Translation of the term "scientific grounds" equates to a recognition that: (1) the assumption is that these disparaged conditions are or may be based in heredity and may be invalid (or, to be more conservative, the hypothesis has not yet achieved established confirmation); and (2) the judgments made by "experts" about a given "abnormal" person, e.g. a mentally retarded person, procreating more "abnormals" apparently varies between professionals; i.e. there is poor reliability.

## SUMMARY

This chapter has focused on how the rights of the mentally retarded are frequently dealt with in a manner different from the rights of the general population, i.e. the non-mentally retarded. Of special concern, there are a number of rights to which, by virtue of the handicapping condition, the mentally retarded person is entitled, such as guardianship, protective services, and treatment. Repeated examples have been cited that show how the reliability concept enters into the circumstances.

CHAPTER SEVEN

# THE LIABILITY OF THE MENTALLY RETARDED

According to the democratic process, if a person is entitled to rights in a society, the person is also subject to a societal expectation of liability. In Chapter Six, one of the primary messages was that the condition of mental retardation does not constitute a justifiable reason to void rights. Likewise, one of the primary messages of this chapter is that the condition of mental retardation does not automatically mean that there should or should not be liability. In other words, mental retardation does not negate responsibility for actions, but there are some logical and justifiable extenuating circumstances that do emanate from the mentally retarded condition.

## RATIONALE FOR EXCEPTION

Stated simply, there is the possibility that an "abnormal" mental condition or mental "defect" might be justification for special consideration in the weighing of liability, such as in judicial proceedings: "The basic *mens rea* concept, the notion that one has not violated the law unless he knows or in some cases should know the facts making his conduct criminal, is the most notable device to excuse those who are thought not blameworthy." (Livermore and Meehl, 1967.) Most famous (or infamous perhaps) is the plea of "not guilty because of insanity." Such a plea has typically been used primarily in cases of alleged capital offenses.

There are, of course, other more rational reasons why a person might, indeed, be exempted from or be accorded an exceptional degree of liability. Through the years, several models or sets of rules (e.g. the *M'Naghten* Model and the *Durham* Model) have been used in law (these will be discussed in a subsequent section). Of concern to this discussion, of course, is how these models and their manifest practices are relevant to the legal aspects of mental retardation. To enter into this analysis, a review of the underlying theoretical principles is necessary.

As might be anticipated, the rationale for exception has a multifaceted composition. The most basic premise is that such consideration would distinguish between offenders who are, in fact, "psychologically innocent" and those who are "psychologically guilty." The connotation is that the latter would, therefore, be subject to punishment, while the former (hopefully) would be treated differently, such as being afforded rehabilitation or some form of therapeutic intervention. Summarily, it is a matter of judging blameworthiness and implementing practices to effect desired social ends.

The term "blameworthiness" may be too elementary to capture the total thrust. Its most pronounced attribute (or liability) is retribution, but as Livermore and Meehl (1967) point out, it goes beyond this level:

> Moreover, the exaction of retribution in more than the hangover from our barbaric past that most observers choose to characterize it. The utility of the criminal law inheres not only in those simplistic notions of deterrence, restraint, and rehabilitation already described. It is based, too, on the creation of an effective individual abhorrence of certain conduct than the largely fictional intellectual balancing of relative pain of imprisonment against pleasure of engaging in a forbidden act. That instinctive aversion is created by viewing criminal conviction as a societal judgment of moral condemnation. By allowing the rest of society to view the criminal as wicked and deserving of punishment, emulation of the criminal's conduct is discouraged.

This prefacing set toward the negative modeling that is promoted is followed by a much more positive objective: "Another related function of the criminal law is the promotion of a sense of individual responsibility for the effects of one's conduct on others." This objective moves directly to a posture that behavioral science can support on philosophical, theoretical, and technical grounds.

The promotion of responsibility has to be the buttressing ingredient for societal development, and it can only be derived from structural contributions that reach down to the individual level. Therefore, one of the foremost concerns of those in societally responsible positions, such as professionals is the "helping" areas, must be the cultivation of responsibility within individuals. It is against this backdrop that the possibility of exception from liability for the mentally retarded (and the mentally ill as well) must be considered.

Although most of the ensuing discussion (throughout this chapter) will be on the possible relationship between the mental condition and the alleged offense, there is also another issue relevant to the mentally retarded: *Competency to stand trial.* Stated in brief, the alleged offender must possess competency to enter into the legal proceedings, such as a trial and possibly the resulting sentencing. Hess, Pearsall, Slichter, and Thomas (1968) state: "It was the rule of common law that an accused could not be required to plead to an indictment or be tried for a crime when he was so mentally disordered that he could not meet the common law tests of competency; that is, when he could not understand the nature and object of the proceedings against him, comprehend his own condition in reference to such proceedings, and assist in his defense." (Note that this statement was based on Michigan law.) The issue of competency to stand trial could be applicable to persons who are mentally retarded and/or mentally ill. In situations of this nature, competency examinations may be ordered; and Hess, Pearsall, Slichter, and Thomas (1968) point out that typically ". . . the judge was free to use any method for determining the accused's competency which was 'discrete and convenient.' " Parenthetically, the preceding two brief quotes readily reveal the subjectivity, and thus the possibility for unreliable proceedings, in such competency actions. Continuing with the procedures for determining competency, if a person were found incompetent to stand trial, presumably he could be assigned to receive a therapeutic intervention (such as being placed in a mental hospital) or he could be confined to jail; he would presumably be tried when, and if, he attained a degree of competency adequate to stand trial.

Returning to exception from liability because of "insanity," Livermore and Meehl (1967) state: "First, the disposition of the offender is irrelevant to the issue of whether one has committed an offense. Yet, the insanity defense is used to negate criminal guilt. Second, no proponent of a test of criminal responsibility seriously contends that his test resolves appropriate disposition. And it would be burdensome to the administration of criminal justice to inject that issue in a meaningful way into a criminal trial."

They continue:

> The major objection to destruction of the insanity defense in favor of confining insanity to resolution of the disposition question is that it would either permit the assessment of moral blame where it is inappropriate or cut loose the criminal law from its moorings of condemnation for moral failure. Once one has started down this road, there is no defensible stopping point short of strict liability with the question of culpability being raised at the stage of disposition. While it is possible to construct a new system, and perhaps a more rational one, on these lines, we assume that such radical reconstruction is neither imminent nor appropriate so long as present social attitudes toward criminals and toward the utilitarian functions of the criminal law continue.

Using a series of cases as exemplary evidence, Livermore and Meehl (1967) defend the *M'Naghten* rule, maintaining that it, "with its focus on cognitive impairment is sounder from the standpoints of the purposes of the criminal law, of present psychiatric knowledge, and of ease of judicial administration than any of the newer tests."

The foregoing material introduces the matter of a mental condition being the basis for exception from liability. Beyond the issue of a defendant's competence to stand trial, there is a major issue of the relevance of his mental condition to the alleged violation or criminal act. The following section will give additional clarity to the rationale by elaborating upon the various models or sets of rules that have been applied.

## MODELS OR RULES

Before entering into any discussion of liability relevant to any form of mental condition, recognition should be given to primary two models or rules that have been most commonly applied in judicial actions; the *M'Naghten* Model and the *Durham* Model.

> The *M'Naghten* rules came from England in 1943, and require that: . . . the jurors ought to be told in all cases that every man is to be presumed to be sane, and to possess a *sufficient degree of reason* to be responsible for his crimes, until the contrary be proved to their satisfaction; and that, to be *clearly* proved that, at the time of the committing of the act, the party accused was labouring under *such* a defect of reason, *from disease of the mind,* as not to know the nature and quality of the act he was doing; or, if he did know it, that he did not know he was doing what was wrong. . . . The usual course therefore has been to leave the question to the jury whether the accused had a *sufficient degree* of reason to know he was doing an act that was wrong . . . (quoted from and italics supplied by Glueck, 1966).

Hinkle (1964) analyzed the *M'Naghten* rule or model and notes that: "This dictum has since been referred to as the 'right and wrong test.' " Robitscher (1966) discusses the *M'Naghten* rule: "The rule states that insanity in itself is not a defense, and that the accused must be more than merely insane to receive a verdict of not guilty by reason of insanity." He continues: "The *M'Naghten* rule holds that a delusion excuses the commission of the crime provided that the situation assumed by the delusion would excuse if the delusion were in fact true, but that the delusion is not an excuse provided the situation assumed by the delusion would not excuse if it were a fact." And he notes: "It still remains the chief test in England—except in some homicide cases where the principle of diminished responsibility applies—and it is the sole test in more jurisdictions of the United States."

The *Durham* rule or model is somewhat more clearcut, at least on the surface; it: ". . . abrogates the right or wrong formula and substitutes the rule that a defendant must be held not guilty if the jury finds that his act was the product of mental disease or defect" (Robitscher, 1966). In contrasting the *M'Naghten* and *Durham* rules, Robitscher (1966) points out: "The *M'Naghten* rule was designed not to define insanity but only to mark out from the larger group of defendants with symptoms of mental illness a smaller group so irrational that they should be relieved of criminal responsibility"; regarding the *Durham* rule he states:

> If *Durham* says that in the light of the impact of psychiatric knowledge of contemporary morality this formula no longer represents social morals, and that today seriously disturbed offenders should not suffer the stigma of criminal conviction but be hospitalized instead of jailed, then it seeks to revolutionize concepts of criminal responsibility rather than modernize a definition to accommodate a wider scope of psychiatric testimony. Under this view, most prisoners—being character neurotics and psychopathic personalities—should be reclassified as patients.

Hinkle (1964) seems prone to retain the *M'Naghten* rule, but to supplement it with "improved and diversified institutional treatment programs for the offender."

A third, more recently emerging, model may be found in the Model Penal Code provided by the American Law Institute; it provides:

1. A person is not responsible for criminal conduct if at the time of such conduct as a result of mental disease or defect he lacks substantial capacity either to appreciate the criminality of his conduct or to conform his conduct to the requirements of law.
2. The terms "mental disease or defect" do not include an abnormality manifested only by repeated criminal or otherwise antisocial conduct. (Robitscher, 1966.)

The Model Penal Code may be interpreted as representing a contemporary movement toward integration of previous models, but there is obviously a lack of specificity.

The criticism of a lack of specificity could easily be applied to all of the existing models of liability relevant to mental conditions. As scrutiny of the foregoing definitions will readily reveal, nebulous phraseology and ambiguous wordings contribute to making the accomplishment of reliability difficult, to say the least.

In the situation with the *Durham* rule, Hofling (1972) points out that courts tend to view the *Durham* rule as being: ". . . unworkable because of the extreme latitude it gives to psychiatric and other medical testimony in the area of value judgments before a jury." And as is relevant to the just mentioned lack of specificity and nebulous language properties, he comments: "As for the vagueness, it is clearly the court's opinion that clarification of what is substantial in any particular case be left to the common sense of the jurors after they have heard the relevant psychiatric and other medical testimony." If lay jurors are left to interpret the professional terminologies used within the contexts of rules that are vague to start with, one can only expect a very unreliable outcome. But this assertion is more than speculation; there are clearcut examples of vagaries.

Reverting back to Glueck's statement (1966) on the *M'Naghten* rule, it was mentioned that he had added the emphasis to selected words; these emphasized or italicized words are apt examples of how reliability could falter. It seems highly likely that expert interpretations of these emphasized words would differ; consequently, the opinions rendered would differ.

The other evident loophole in attaining reliability is the mere fact that there is no agreement on which, if any, of the rules or models should be applied. Even more specific, each rule or model is predicated on the hypothesis that there is such an entity as mental illness and that it can be validly and reliably ascertained; but the discussions of diagnosis in Chapter Three and nosology in Chapter Four emphasize that this hypothesis has not been adequately substantiated.

Lest there be any misunderstanding, many of the citations herein are directed primarily toward mentally ill persons, but the terminology used (such as "defect of reason") permits these same rules or models to be applied, rightly or wrongly, to mentally retarded persons.

## SOCIETAL PRAGMATISM

The fixing of responsibility, which is the implicit objective within all of the foregoing rules and which is welded to the subsequent discussion of liability, is, like it or not, a societal mandate. It is an issue on which legal professionals and the lay public as well must reach some common ground for agreement. Robitscher (1966) argues against extreme change, stating:

> First, unless some extreme position is drawn—for instance, unless all offenders are considered ill, or no offenders are considered, or the defense of insanity is abolished—the question of the legal responsibility of the defendant will be at issue, which will in our tradition involve questions concerning his state of mind and extent of control over his

own actions. Whether liberal or narrow concepts of mental illness prevail will then depend not entirely on the wording of the "test" or "rule": the emotional climate prevailing in society, the philosophy of the judge, the prejudices of the jury will continue to be more important than the wording of the "test." In a peaceful and prosperous society, the emphasis will probably shift toward rehabilitation and less emphasis on guilt; in a threatened society, the emphasis will shift towards punishment and deterrence. Economic factors, the tensions prevailing in society, the extent of knowledge, the understanding in society of psychiatric concepts, the concepts of what society is trying to accomplish—all these are more important than the wording of a "test."

The message regarding reliability is pronounced: there can be no fixed reliable system for determining responsibility when an "abnormal" mental condition is allegedly involved, because the decision-making processes and the decision-makers themselves are subjected to a myriad of ever changing, intervening variables. The only consolation found within behavioral science for this inability to assure reliable processing (and admittedly it is small consolation from a humanistic vantage point) is found in three of Thorne's (1961) postulates on the nature of clinical judgment:

*The ethical justification for making a clinical judgment which does not have complete scientific support and validation is that it only professes to be the best that can be offered at time and place.*

*Clinical decisions must inevitably reflect expedience in many situations where there are no scientifically valid bases for decision or where there are conflicts of value systems all of which have some "rightness."*

*Even in view of the admitted invalidity or relative inefficiency of many clinical decisions, society must depend upon clinical decisions. because of the practical and economic limitations of life situations.*

These are exactly the kinds of assumptions that provide a rationale for a legal system that functions in an unreliable manner. The individual is left to ponder whether *societal pragmatism* is or is not adequate justification for maintenance of an acknowledged faulty system.

## LIABILITY

In turning to liability, there appear to be two models of criminal liability: the subjective and the objective. Regarding the subjective, Dix (1971) states:

> The subjective model emphasizes the characteristics of the particular offender. Liability is properly imposed only if it is established that (1) the individual has violated or endangered a social interest, (2) the individual's actions or failure to act violated a rule of which the offender was aware, (3) the offender himself acknowledged at the time that this rule "should" have been obeyed, and (4) the offender's decision to violate the rule was not significantly influenced by factors other than the philosophical decision to violate the norm. This model, of course, emphasizes "moral culpability" by authorizing liability only when the offender has voluntarily, in the broadest sense of the word, violated a norm which he himself recognized as deserving his adherence.

For the objective model, Dix (1971) indicates: "The objective model, on the other hand, emphasizes the threat which an individual poses directly to social interests protected by criminal sanctions. Liability is properly imposed if the individual in fact has demonstrated that he poses a threat to social interests, that is, if it established that the individual has, by his actions or omissions, violated or endangered a social interest." Dix adds: "The objective model may rest upon acceptance of the retributive justification for punishment: punishment is justified if the individual has caused danger or danger that the law prohibits." Analyzing both the subjective and objective models should reveal that both are, in fact, subjective; in other words, value judgments, with all of their inherent covert and overt vulnerabilities to biases, have to be made to apply to either model.

Any discussion of liability must give early consideration to the subject of *torts*. Gatti and Gatti (1972) provide a brief definition:

> If one commits a crime, he has broken a law against society. If one commits a tort, he has broken a law against an individual. People have the right to be free from physical and mental injury. They have the right to be secure and feel secure in their life, liberty and property. Therefore, all people owe all other people the duty of not infringing upon these rights. If a person violates that duty, the injured party has the right to be reimbursed for any injury caused by the violation.

They indicate that a tort consists of four ingredients:

1. "*Duty*. The duty to respect other people's rights.

2. "*Violation.* The breaking of that duty owed to another person.
3. "*Cause.* The violation of another's rights having caused injury to that person.
4. "*Injury.* The person violated being injured mentally or physically."

Obviously a tort could be committed intentionally, but negligence is also a tort. Of concern in this book is the possible relationship of mental factors to a tort.

Curran (1960) has examined tort liability relevant to the mentally ill and mentally deficient. He acknowledges that, regarding tort law in general, there are at least four "striking features"; they are:

1. The courts are treating nearly all torts alike in denying a defense of mental disease.
2. The reasons for holding liability are policy matters having little to do with theory of the different torts or an analysis of mental disease.
3. There has been almost no attempt to define what is meant by "insanity" in tort cases.
4. There are surprisingly few cases in American law in which an insanity defense has been raised.

He augments these four characteristics with the following comments:

> The characteristics indicated above are to a great extent interlocked as a rationale in the individual decisions we have examined. The fact that the reasons for holding liability apply equally to all torts leads the courts to ignore distinctions in the required elements of the torts. Since they deny the defense rather summarily, they do not feel the need to analyze or define "insanity." Yet, it seems to me that if the *number* of cases increase, our modern courts under the pressure of better-presented and better-argued defenses may be forced to entertain at least an examination of the distinctions drawn above.

And he continues:

> In the criminal law, a consistent theory of responsibility can be maintained. The theories of responsibility in torts, however, are too divergent to allow such a practice to be easily maintained. To illustrate this point, it seems to me that in the case law previously examined the most significant developments have been in defamation and negli-

gence. In defamation, two important cases have allowed a defense of insanity where the defamatory remarks were the result of deluded thinking. This same theory could be applied to other torts such as malicious prosecution and abuse of civil process where the defendants act under paranoid delusions.

Curran (1960) seems to believe (at least at the time of his publication) that criminal courts have been less than favorable toward defense of insanity in tort cases, and he cites four theories or reasons why courts have tended to deny the defense of insanity in tort cases:

1. Tort law, unlike criminal law, is predicated on compensating for harm done, not inflicting punishment. It looks to the act of the defendant and its resultant harm, not to guilty intent.
2. As between the insane actor who caused the harm and his innocent victim, the tort law looks with favor on the victim. It will require that the insane person compensate the victim from his available estate rather than allow the loss to fall wholly on the victim.
3. The imposing of liability on the insane persons will encourage custodians and guardians of the insane to prevent their wards from inflicting harm on others.
4. Were a rule of non-responsibility for the insane to be adopted, it could be used as a fraudulent defense since the absence of mental illness may be difficult to prove.

The foregoing is, of course, directed ostensibly at the "insane," and one is left to conjecture as to how applicable these points are to the "mentally retarded." In view of other similarities between the "insane" and the "mentally retarded" raised in Curran's (1960) review, it would appear that these theories and the logical guidelines that could be deduced would be applicable to the mentally retarded. More will be said shortly about distinctions between persons with mental illness and mental retardation relevant to tort liability.

In view of the prominence of contracts in regard to the rights of the mentally retarded, brief mention should be made of the liability of the mentally retarded in this area. Based on Australian law, Bray (1971) indicates that: ". . . the ordinary contracts of a person of unsound mind will still be binding on him if the other party did not know about his disability and was not aware of any circumstances from which he ought to have inferred it. In other words, even a man who, by reason of his mental condition, does not understand the nature of the contract into which he is entering will be bound by it if the other party did not know about the mental unsoundness and had no reason to suspect it." This type of contract liability does, of course, support the need for effective guardianship for some mentally retarded persons.

On the issue of distinctions between mental deficiency and mental illness relevant to tort liability, Curran (1960) states the following about mental deficiency:

> We might start our examination with the basic distinction between mental illness and mental deficiency. Some of the case law has lumped the two under "insanity." By mental deficiency we mean an abnormally low level of *intelligence* according to the age of the individual. It is caused by an arrested or imperfect development in the brain itself usually congenital in origin, but sometimes the result of disease or trauma. The degree of mental deficiency can be measured fairly accurately by intelligence quotient tests and is roughly graded severe, moderate, or mild. Severely or moderately deficient persons are apt to be institutionalized or otherwise only remotely in contact with community life. Many of the mildly deficient or persons of borderline intelligence may, however, be able to function in everyday life if heavy demands and responsibilities are not placed on them. Functioning in such a way, their low intelligence is often unrecognized. Such persons are amenable to basic social controls and moral standards. They can control their conduct. The law usually deals with them as normal persons and this seems a quite sensible approach.

Note that this rather lengthy statement, while primarily for the purpose of introducing tort liability considerations, was included because of the sensitive definition for mental retardation as would be applicable to tort liability that it provides.

Moving more directly to the issue of tort liability, Curran (1960) states:

> It would seem likely that any defense of mental deficiency in a tort action would be limited to the lower levels of the categories of deficiency. Even in these situations, however, I would guess that the judges would be reluctant to draw lines of liability and non-liability based on rigid IQ levels. They would fall back on traditional concepts such as "capacity" and "intent" and would ask the expert witnesses to

> testify in these terms. For mental deficiency, at least, the result would be a test somewhat similar to that used for minors. An argument along these lines has more chance of success and, I believe, greater psychiatric validity, than the older plea to extend the subjective test for minors to all "insane persons."

Curran (1960) ends his authoritative review with the following conclusion:

> The issue of the tort liability of mentally ill and mentally deficient persons depends on considerations of tort theory, social policy, and the realities of mental disease in our society. At present the social policy of holding liability dominates in the common law courts of this country. The tort theory of responsibility in this area is not as yet resolved, however, while the realities of mental disease are not clearly presented and understood. Until such time as these factors have been measured and evaluated in the decisions, the future course of liability must be considered uncertain.

As Curran so aptly states in the immediately preceding quote, the uncertainties about mental conditions and the unresolved tort theory of responsibility when a mental condition is involved can only be interpreted as an indication that mentally retarded persons involved in tort law cases cannot be assured of reliable dealings.

In probably most liability cases involving mentally retarded persons, considerable emphasis is placed on measured intelligence. This was reflected in several ways within the previously cited quotes from Curran's (1960) review; but as Curran cautioned, it seems likely that ". . . judges would be reluctant to draw lines of liability and nonliability based on rigid IQ levels." This is still another issue, however, that is not settled, because there are advocates for the belief that measured intelligence should be influential in the determination of liability. Hinkle (1959) provided a historical account of laws relevant to criminal responsibility (particularly those applicable to children), and noted: "Early in the law it was recognized that idiocy was a factor negating criminal responsibility, with complete ignorance as its hall-mark." His views on the criminal liability of mentally retarded persons place strong emphasis on measured intelligence: "It would seem reasonable to expect that with the advent of intelligence tests there would be a significant impact with respect to ascertaining responsibility of those with low mentality. While 'intelligence' and 'criminal capacity' are obviously not synonymous it would seem that a measure of the intelligence of a defendant in any criminal action in which the capacity to formulate or entertain the intent required in the particular act for which he is on trial should be an important aid to the jury or judge determining the matter." The point, therefore, is that the theory of liability relevant to people with "abnormal" mental conditions finds no definitive support from an agreement about what role, if any, intelligence should play in the determination of liability.

CHAPTER EIGHT

# ADMINISTRATIVE AND JUDICIAL PROCEDURES FOR THE MENTALLY RETARDED

THE TOPIC OF THIS CHAPTER, the administrative and judicial procedures for the mentally retarded, encompasses most of the material presented throughout this book. After all, the administrative and judicial procedures or processing represent the culmination of all the efforts from other sources to the legal aspects of mental retardation.

The focus of this chapter will be on providing selected examples of administrative and judicial procedures relevant to the mentally retarded. Although similar to previously presented material, these procedures to be discussed should be viewed as constituting a general frame of reference for considering (evaluating?) the efficacy (or lack of it) inherent to legal procedures, manifested in administrative and judicial actions, for the mentally retarded.

## HANDLING MENTALLY DISORDERED BEHAVIOR

An initial issue that first appears philosophical but readily evolves into practical administrative actions is the contemporary approach to handling mentally disordered behavior. That is, statutes are moving responsibility for the mentally disordered to the community level and thus there are varying ways in which commitment, particularly involuntary commitment, can be handled. Based on the Community Mental Health Services Law in California, Abramson (1972) notes:

> The criteria for initial involuntary treatment were made more stringent, and a graded series of standards was established; it requires the demonstration of increasingly severe impairment or dangerousness from mental disorder or chronic alcoholism in order to justify longer

periods of involuntary detention and treatment. In general, these longer periods of involuntary treatment follow mandatory judicial hearings. In contrast, the initial, shorter periods merely require a less formal mental health certification procedure, with formal judicial hearings only on request of the patient.

While the intent of these laws was ". . . to increase the legal rights and reduce the legal disabilities of mentally ill persons involuntarily detained and treated in mental hospitals"—certainly an honorable intention—there may well be societal factors that lead to less positive effects. Specifically, if the laws governing commitment, particularly involuntary commitment, become all *too* lenient, i.e. do not allow mental health professionals time to diagnose properly and to treat the involuntary patient, he may return to the community and provoke reactions that could eventuate in a greater disadvantage to him than had he been involuntarily maintained for a longer period. Abramson (1972) states: "There may be a limit to society's tolerance of mentally disordered behavior. If the entry of persons exhibiting mentally disordered behavior into the mental health system of social control is impeded, community pressure will force them into the criminal justice system of social control. Further, if the mental health system is forced to release mentally disordered persons into the community prematurely, there will be an increase in pressure for the use of the criminal justice system to reinstitutionalize them."

Abramson (1972) further clarifies the message: "Police seem to be aware of the more stringent criteria under which mental health professionals are now accepting responsibility for involuntary detention and treatment, and thus regard arrest and booking into jail as a more reliable way of securing involuntary detention of mentally disordered persons."

Stated most succinctly, if laws relevant to involuntary and voluntary commitment do not maintain both the rights of the potential patient (which would include the allowance of adequate time for effective diagnostic and therapeutic interventions during the commitment) and the rights of society, the end result could be: *the criminalization of mentally disordered behavior!* In other words, society's administrative vehicles, such as the police department, would receive preference. The term "mentally disordered" is probably more closely aligned with "mental illness" than "mental retardation," but—and as has so often been the case—it is highly likely that mentally retarded persons would be affected in the same manner. Again, it is an example of how unreliable treatment of the mentally retarded could result from ineffectual administrative/legal conditions.

## JURY ACTIONS

For those mentally retarded persons subjected to judicial services, there is the issue of "judgment being passed by one's peers." A lengthy debate could ensue, undoubtedly to no avail, about the letter of the law, which theoretically might allow for juries to be composed of mentally retarded persons if the defendant were mentally retarded. Such debate would be an exercise in futility; but it is, parenthetically, interesting to note that a recent well-publicized situation involved mentally healthy professionals voluntarily admitting themselves to mental hospitals. Despite their actually being of a healthy mental status, they went unrecognized by the professionals in the hospitals; *however,* some of the real mental patients detected that the pseudo-patients were different!

The matter regarding jury selection for the mentally retarded is illustrated in the following study. Strodtbeck, Simon, and Hawkins (1970), using real jury members, conducted mock juries in order to study the effects of status (such as employment status) in jury deliberations; their findings were: "Jury deliberations have been used to examine the intersection of occupational status and sex with the typically small-group measures of participation, influence, satisfaction, and perceived competence. The assumption that there is no relationship between these modes of classification can be safely rejected. Men, in contrast with women, and persons of higher status, in contrast with lower status occupations, have higher participation influence, satisfaction, and perceived competence for the jury task."

The point is, since the typical layman (and, alas, many professionals) has special feelings about people with deviancies, as the mentally retarded person would undoubtedly get classified, jury selection should involve assessment of sociological and psychological factors that might be relevant to decision-making about a mentally retarded person. As the previous study indicated, sociological variables do influence outcome, and there seems to be no reason to believe that jury deliberations about a mentally retarded person would be exempt from such a sociological principle. The issue of reliability could be exemplified if an unscreened jury and a jury whose members had been screened about their attitudes toward mentally retarded persons deliberated about the same mentally retarded individual. Sociological theory would support the probability of different deliberation elements and the possibility even of a different outcome decision, not because of facts but because of jury members' attitudes toward and/or reactions to the mental retardation.

## LEGAL REPRESENTATION

Previous mention has been made of the right to legal representation. In the context of the Australian Mental Health Act, Bray (1971) points out that the mental status of the person influences his legal representation:

> Special precautions surround the position of a person of unsound mind in civil litigation. The rules of the Supreme Court, for example, provide that a mental defective can only bring or defend proceedings by a best friend or guardian *ad litem*. . . . It might be added that the authority of a solicitor to act on behalf of his client ceases when the client becomes of unsound mind, whether the solicitor knows about it or not, and he might find himself personally liable to the other party for costs if he continues to act in the name of his client after he has become insane.

Closer to home perhaps, Brown and Courtless (1968) found that of thirty-one inmates, two did not have legal counsel; seventeen pleaded guilty; twenty gave confessions or incriminating statements before the trial; and only three had retardation raised as an issue in the hearing prior to the conviction, and there were no pretrial examinations on the other twenty-eight. Overall, even though this group was subsequently identified (while in prison) as being mentally retarded, presentencing examinations were done on only six of the thirty-one. These data obviously relate to the material that will subsequently be presented on judicial handling, but they also raise the question: What if these mentally retarded persons had effective legal counsel? More will be said about legal counsel, but suffice it to say that the lack of legal counsel no doubt influenced the reliability of the proceedings.

## GUARDIANSHIP

The important role that guardianship, as discussed in detail in Chapter Six, plays with so many mentally retarded persons merits special mention. Regarding reliability of the need for guardianship, apparently there is a marked void in the law for this area. Ober (1963) states: "There is no reference in the literature that there be incorporated into the statutes for the mentally retarded provisions for continuing or periodic evaluations in respect to incompetence." Surely the pursuit of reliable usage of guardianship would require periodic, thorough evaluations of the need for such guardianship.

## TREATMENT

The right to treatment has been discussed extensively in Chapter Six. From an administrative/judicial viewpoint, the study of the mentally retarded in penal and correctional institutions conducted by Brown and Courtless (1968) revealed that 56 percent of the institutions had no special programs for the mentally retarded, and only 4.5 percent of the institutions had comprehensive programs (including psychotherapy) for the mentally retarded. Bazelon (1969) underscores two important points. First, the mere provision of services is not enough (although that might be an improvement over the present situation); the services must be effective: "The most important facet of the right to treatment is not that the hospital does something for everyone, but that it does the right thing for the right patient. . . . Any legislative definition of adequate treatment should therefore insure not only that the hospital provides treatment in general, but also that it tailors the treatment offered to the specific patient."

Second, while constructive actions within a particular (i.e. singular) institution or socio-political pressures brought to bear on a particular administrative/judicial source might produce valuable but isolated results, the end conclusion is that legislation must be enacted: ". . . courts cannot implement the right without the aid of a legislative framework." The reliability of fulfilling the right to treatment for the mentally retarded, therefore, necessitates a prefacing set that encompasses effective legal counsel, consideration of the mental retardation state during the proceedings, and then a placement source that actually has services that accommodate the mental retardation in general and meets the mentally retarded individual's idiosyncratic characteristics in specific.

## JUDICIAL HANDLING

A final area in the administrative/judicial processes is almost exclusively within the realm of judicial handling. The most basic ingredient, perhaps, is acknowledging that the defendant is, in fact, mentally retarded, with the assumption being that the judicial proceedings will then give some consideration to the issue of mental retardation in the deliberations. Brown, Courtless, and Silber (1970), in their study of mentally retarded offenders, commented that there was: ". . . the almost total failure to identify the men in our sample as retarded at any time prior to their admission to prison." Further, they reveal that several judges and prosecutors interviewed: ". . . stated that they were surprised to learn that the subjects they had tried, or prosecuted, were retarded. They said they saw no evidence before or during the trial to suggest these defendants were significantly impaired intellectually."

Relatedly, whether the mentally retarded person had been so identified or not, the fact that he was mentally retarded, even if only later established during a prison testing program, would seemingly contradict the reliability of his judicial proceedings. For example, Bazelon (1968) points out that confessions from mentally retarded persons are unreliable and a similar position cited previously is maintained by Haggerty, Kane, and Udall (1972). The "California Study" conducted by Kay, Farnham, Karren, Knakal, and Diamond (1972) is filled with data that could almost lead to labeling the study "Unreliable Judicial Handling of the Mentally Retarded." The major point was that the California system was inexcusably and inexhaustibly inconsistent. For example, it was pointed out that persons with quite different educational backgrounds performed the same functions in the commitment of the mentally retarded (and presumably effective judicial handling should have some relevance to specific areas of academic competence). They noted that there was no uniform practice as to "whether the local agent actually saw the allegedly retarded person during the commitment and application process," there again supporting an unreliable procedure. They found that no judge ever refused to commit; i.e. they had never refused a commitment order, and the hospital's decision to accept the mentally retarded person was the most influential factor in the judicial decision. The majority of the judges acknowledged that they were a "rubberstamp" for the others' decisions (and it was noted that hearings rarely lasted more than 5 or 10 minutes). While commitments were apparently made with great speed, there were no provisions for "restoration to competence" in the statutes. Indeed, they note that the only point of unanimity among those persons who worked with the commitment of the mentally retarded was that no agent maintained contact with the case, such as with either the alleged mentally retarded person or their family, after the court hearing. All of the foregoing factors can be interpreted as supporting a hodge-podge of ineffectual case handling that could hardly accomplish a reliable means for commitment of the mentally retarded. Parenthetically, the one bright note is that Kay, Farnham, Karren, Knakal, and Diamond (1972) cite several proposals and actions being implemented that should contradict the preceding conglomeration of unreliable administrative and judicial processes.

CHAPTER NINE

# EXPERT TESTIMONY FOR THE MENTALLY RETARDED

ONE OF THE MOST rapidly expanding practices within legal services, particularly for persons with what are assumed to be "other than normal" mental conditions, is the use of expert witnesses. That is, professionals are brought into legal proceedings to issue, based on their learned statures, opinions about the relevance of specific factors or conditions to the alleged offense.

In situations involving a mental condition, the expert testimony is, of course, designed to contribute to a defense or prosecution that has encompassed pleas of insanity or diminished responsibility (such as was discussed in Chapter Eight in the material on the *M'Naghten* and *Durham* rules). For further clarity, an analogy is present in medicine; for example, medico-legal cases might involve a medical physician to "establish," via his expert opinion, the presence or absence of a physical condition, e.g. a physical handicap or disability, and the relationship between it and an action or set of circumstances that were alleged to have contributed to or caused the physical condition. In other words, it would be for establishing liability.

This chapter will, naturally, focus primarily on the use of expert or professional testimony for legal aspects of retardation. It is important to note that most of the attention devoted to expert testimony is within the realm of criminal and tort law, but there are other non-criminal or non-offense oriented situations that the professional can and should become involved in via providing expert testimony for the mentally retarded. Some of these instances move directly toward *advocacy* (an issue that will receive further consideration in Chapter Ten), but many of them could be more properly labeled "administrative"; that is, it is a matter of expert witnesses being mustered to assure that the rights of the mentally retarded are upheld in everyday life. The issue of reliability will, of course, be interwoven throughout this chapter.

## THE PHILOSOPHY OF EXPERT TESTIMONY

Although the pragmatic usage may be of most interest, there are also philosophical considerations. Glueck (1966) indicates:

> Though usually only implicit, the freedom-determination issue is fundamental to criminal law and penology; it is basic in designing an acceptable practical "test" of irresponsibility where it is claimed the defendant was mentally ill at the time of the crime, and it is involved, consequently, in delimiting the scope of admissible psychiatric testimony and in defining the role of the jury in the assessment of guilt or innocence. The reason for this multiform realistic significance of the free will-determinism argumentation is that it contributes heavily to the definition of the water-shed between those who stress the prime social need of blameworthiness and retributive punishment as the core-concept in crime and justice and those who, under the impact of psychiatric, psychoanalytic, sociological, and anthropological views, insist that man's choices are the product of forces largely beyond his conscious control, and that simply to blame and punish is neither to understand nor to cure the offender, nor in the long run to protect society.

Further on the philosophical underpinnings of the use of expert testimony, Dix (1971) states: "Nor does it necessarily follow that consideration of psychological abnormality is consistent with utilitarian policy. There is a lack of evidence that psychological abnormality renders an individual significantly less subject to the preventive function of the threat of criminal punishment. In fact, even if the assumptions of the psychodynamic psychologists are accepted, it is still reasonable to expect that the unconscious may be influenced by the experience that those who commit antisocial acts are punished."

And he continues:

> On balance, the arguments in favor of considering psychological abnormality seem persuasive. Whatever the present limitation on accurately determining the psychological dynamics of particular offenders, the situation is likely to improve with practice. Mental

health professionals, engaged in the treatment process, seldom have the opportunity to speculate concerning the mental processes of an offender as they relate to the criminal law. If the law expects such professionals to be of more help than they have been in the past, it must provide the opportunity for them to practice their analysis. Perhaps this is where the greatest value of the concept lies: it encourages courts, the general public, and mental health personnel to address themselves not only to broad questions of crime prevention and general philosophical issues related to punishment, but also to the problem of the specific offender and what should be done in "this case." From continued experimentation in this area, it is reasonable to expect the development of a more sophisticated ability to analyze particular cases as well as the development of a body of knowledge on which to build a more realistic substantive criminal law.

These quotes are intended to illustrate that the involvement of mental health professionals in legal processes, as might be manifested in expert testimony, has ramifications that extend much beyond a particular person going through judicial proceedings—the involvement moves to a societal recognition of responsibility for the commitment of criminal (and other) acts and the forms of retribution or "penance" that should be enforced.

## EXPERT TESTIMONY FOR LIABILITY

While the overriding issue may be one of whether behavioral scientists (which would include medical personnel) should be involved in legal processes in any way, shape, or form—such as conducting research on the legal procedures—the most basic issue is whether they should use their professional expertise to evaluate a defendant and made a "professional opinion" that would be accepted as evidence for consideration in the guilt or innocence issue.

In the case of persons with unusual or abnormal mental conditions, the initially accepted expert testimony was solely from psychiatrists, the assumption being that their medical training distinguished them for formulating opinions about mental disease or conditions. With shifts in societal attitudes toward mental health and with the increasing amount of impressive empirical support from other mental health specialties, expert testimony was soon accepted from non-physicians, particularly psychologists (Allen, Ferster, and Rubin, 1968). At this point in time, the general "rule of thumb" seems to be that any professional can potentially serve as an "expert witness," but in accepting his statements as creditable evidence, he must establish his credentials. Stated differently, the position now is one where the discipline or academic degree *per se* does not automatically justify the professional providing testimony or opinions that will be accepted into the legal proceedings as evidence; rather, it is his *unique* set of qualifications that must be weighted. This certainly seems to be a step in the right direction, and should, in the process, increase both the validity and reliability of the expert testimony.

There have been many authoritative texts on expert testimony, particularly for purposes of orienting the professional to the role expectations intrinsic to serving as an expert witness in liability proceedings (e.g. Allen, Ferster, and Rubin, 1968; Davidson, 1965). One major point is that the three primary mental health specialties have well-documented places in legal proceedings: the psychiatrist (Davidson, 1965; Robitscher, 1972b), psychology (Kolasa, 1972; Pacht, Kuehn, Bassett, and Nash, 1973; Redmount, 1967), and social work (Hansen and Goldberg, 1967). It is critical to recognize, however, that, and as was stated previously in another form, mere professional stature does not make for an effective, e.g. reliable, expert witness.

Professional stature alone is not enough. Brodsky and Robey (1972) pointedly assert that the effectiveness of the expert witness depends upon awareness of the roles and procedures that accompany a court appearance. From an analysis for delineating a variety of factors to which the effective expert witness must be oriented, they divide the continuum of functions into three states: the pretrial, on the witness stand, and posttrial. The following three quotes from Brodsky and Robey (1972) seem to present an astute, illustrative view of the expert witness stages. For the pretrial stage, they state:

> In the pretrial phase, the attitudes of the courtroom-unfamiliar witness are negative and fearful, and he has some personal and professional fears about active forensic involvement. He usually has little or no training in forensic practices, prepares as if the clinical case were

> to be presented in a professional conference, and has a minimal contact with the attorneys or judicial procedure in advance. On the other hand, the courtroom-oriented witness is frequently a product of legal-psychological training or postgraduate education, is well aware of the legal issues involved, and invests more effort, time, and careful keeping of records than with non-forensic clients. He seeks out extensive evaluation opportunities, is in frequent communication with the attorneys, and prepares a report that may be understood by lay audiences. The courtroom-oriented witness understands the advocacy system, the purpose and nature of expert testimony, and judicial decision-making processes. The courtroom-unfamiliar witness often does not.

In describing the "on the witness stand" stage, they state:

> The witness-stand behavior and attitudes of our two models usually represent sharp contrasts. From the perspective of a juror, the two types may be seen as follows. The courtroom-oriented witness speaks in language that is understandable. This witness instructs while explaining, speaks directly to the jury, and is composed, courteous, and consistent during cross-examination. He readily admits areas of uncertainty and ignorance that exists for himself and his profession. Because of his familiarity with the issues and procedures, he rarely is "boxed in" during cross-examination. On the other hand, the testimony of the courtroom-unfamiliar witness is such that jurors sometimes find it difficult to keep their attention from wandering, at least during direct examination. Such witnesses use technical terms and often stubbornly cling to small points or overstate findings when cross-examined. The perceptive juror will observe the courtroom-unfamiliar witness becoming anxious, sometimes brusque during cross-examination, or amenable to manipulations through semantic or hypothetical questions.

And at the final "posttrial" stage:

> After the testimony is completed, the courtroom-oriented witness usually has positive or at least neutral feelings toward the experience. He frequently receives much positive reinforcement—financially as well as personally—and will continue forensic activities. At the extreme, the courtroom-unfamiliar man often leaves with a sense of anger, will sometimes perceive himself and his views as having been on trial, and now and then will make speeches to professional groups about the unbridgable gap between law and psychology (or psychiatry).

It is believed that Brodsky and Robey's (1972) analysis and set of guidelines (which are deducible from their analytic comments) constitute a valuable lesson for the professional who intends to serve as an expert witness. Stated succinctly, the results of the expert testimony will depend upon three factors: (1) *the quality of the material on which the opinion is based;* (2) *the professional stature (such as in terms of credentials) of the expert witness; and* (3) *the demeanor and communicative skills of the professional during the pretrial, witness stand, and posttrial stages.*

The use of expert witnesses has been far from uncontroversial. Suarez (1972) states:

> The role of expert witness has given rise to a great deal of friction and misunderstanding. Most attorneys and judges still have a dim view of psychiatry, and most psychiatrists assiduously avoid legal involvement, leaving the job to a small band of "professional" experts. The role of the therapist of offenders is largely mythical. Most legalists are convinced that psychiatry and other behavioral sciences have little, if anything, to offer. Most psychiatrists are given very little experience in legal areas in the course of their training and develop little interest in these areas. The jobs themselves are typically unprestigious, unrewarding, and in out-of-the-way locations.

While Suarez (1972) was speaking for the specialty of psychiatry, many of the same attitudes and issues are relevant to the specialty of psychology. Redmount (1967), speaking for the specialty of psychology, states:

> Psychologists, for the most part, have little practical experience with attorneys and with the legal context. Some have served as expert witnesses, and others may have been approached or consulted more informally by attorneys. There are differences in training, interest, attitude, and temperament among psychologists, as there are among attorneys. Likely, factors of personal adjustment, involving matters of attitude and temperament, between a particular attorney and psychologist will determine whether natural professional barriers and biases can be overcome, and whether the psychologist, his skills and his knowledge, can be successfully utilized by the attorney.

This admittedly negative stance, which in all too many instances boils down (as was mentioned) to personality clashes and to a lack of information about the other specialties (e.g. the contributions that each specialty can make), is apparently being rapidly replaced with a more optimistic, interdisciplinary accord.

Robitscher (1972b) goes so far as to assert that there is a "new face of legal psychiatry," and Kolasa (1972) describes a wide variety of new functions that can both contribute positively to the legal proceedings and can make the involvement more attractive to the professional mental health worker.

Reliability is a pronounced concern in the use of expert testimony. Given the highly dubious assumption that the measures will reveal states and traits that do, in fact, exist in a somewhat permanent condition (in other words, given the assumption that the measures are valid), the formulation of opinions leads inevitably to possible variances, i.e. unassured reliability. Robitscher (1970) states: "We are increasingly aware that psychiatric opinion is not as soundly based as most medical opinion—on hard data and laboratory results."

And he notes that some psychiatrists, apparently because of philosophical and professional theoretical reasons, tend to be extremists; he states: "Extremism saves the extremist from the need to make decisions. If all criminals (or no criminals) are mentally ill, the psychiatrist does not have the job of drawing the line to separate the mentally abnormal from the well offender."

He is also aware of social and biological factors that enter into the professional opinions of some expert witnesses, and addresses himself to the reliability issue by saying: "A pragmatic answer is that overburdened courts that do not cope well with our present concepts of organic and psychological bases for exemption from responsibility cannot possibly embrace emerging medical concepts not yet substantiated, refined, and clarified. Some of the factors considered here are too conjectural and too imprecise for courts that have the obligation of handing out reasonably speedy justice in accordance with the articulated standards."

His suggestion would be: "A more humanitarian answer is that, although these factors cannot now be used to excuse, they can be used to temper, and that courts, both in determining sentences and planning methods of rehabilitation of criminals, must be aware of the factors that bear on the capabilities of the individual. Retardation does not necessarily excuse a crime, but it does alter our perspective on the criminal."

The foregoing quotes are in accord with the material in Chapter Eight on the administrative and judicial handling of the mentally retarded, because certainly there is a message regarding how courts should handle mentally retarded persons. But there is also a clearcut message for the issue of expert testimony, namely that professionals who enter into expert testimony must not conceptualize themselves as being the "judge and jury," but as a professional who is offering information to the actual judge and jury to consider; and in keeping with the comprehensive definition of the term "diagnosis," they are professionals who are bound to offer a prognostication that encompasses therapeutic or rehabilitative intervention alternatives.

The professional who provides expert testimony must be careful, as noted in the foregoing paragraph, of being moved into conflicting roles. One of the most conflicting roles would be to serve as an evaluator of the person for whom he will provide expert testimony and then to be, as well, a potential therapist. This is clearly illustrated by Chambers (1972) in discussing the procedures relevant to the insanity defense. He questions whether doctors at a given hospital should be allowed to testify for or against a defendant if it is possible that the defendant might eventually end up in that doctor's hospital. Chambers (1972) states:

> Similarly due process requires that government doctors whose word carries such enormous weight be in a position to render judgment unaffected by factors irrelevant to the question they are asked . . . disqualification seems the only appropriate remedy. First, they are provided by the Government and the Government is held to high standards of fairness in its handling of criminal cases. And second, as shown above, their findings, especially when negative, are so rarely rejected by judges or juries that they can be properly held, because of this *de facto* power, to the standards of impartiality to which we hold the judges themselves.

He goes on to say: "Thus, there remains an important overlap in staff involved in both diagnosis and treatment. Even if a total separation occurred within the hospital, however, institutional pressures—awareness of overcrowding and so forth—might continue to influence the diagnostic process." One solution, according to Chambers (1972), would be to establish public legal services or to require the use of private practitioners.

The conflicting roles of the professional could, quite obviously, affect the reliability (and validity) of both his expert opinion and the judicial decision-making. Chambers (1972) provides further clarification: "Though technically merely advisers to the Court, the hospital doctors effectively make the final decision in the vast majority of insanity defense cases. If the hospital certifies a defendant as not mentally ill, he will in the great majority of cases abandon his effort to establish an insanity defense, even though there may well be other psychiatrists, equally competent, who would believe him seriously ill."

And he delimits two issues within the current practices at St. Elizabeths Hospital in Washington, D.C., that lead to what he believes ". . . results in a denial of liberty without due process of law to anyone found guilty after a trial in which a St. Elizabeths doctor has testified adversely to his defense"; these two issues are:

> First, if a hospital doctor testifies that the defendant is not mentally ill, the factfinder—the judge or jury—may quite justly fear that the hospital will promptly release him if he is found not guilty by reason of insanity. It may thus return a verdict of guilty even though it believes the testimony of other doctors at the hospital or outside doctors that the defendant is seriously ill and deserves acquittal.
>
> Second, the doctors who examine a defendant at St. Elizabeths may be influenced, consciously or unconsciously, in making their diagnosis by the prospect that the defendant will be returned to them if found not guilty by reason of insanity. Given the elusiveness of the notion of mental illness, a doctor may unconsciously resolve a close case not on medical grounds but on the grounds that the defendant would pose difficult control problems for the hospital. . . .

Just as these kinds of factors can influence expert testimony, they can, as was brought out in Chapter Eight, influence the final legal process: the judicial handling.

Another potential form of role conflict may be found in the issue of expert review versus an adversary position. The adversary system involves the best obtainable attorneys for the defense and for the prosecution bringing in the best possible witnesses to oppose each other (even though privately they may have little or no doubt about the truth of testimony from an opposing witness), and attempts will be made to cross-examine and to discredit the witnesses from the opposing side—and, of course, a group of laymen, i.e. the jury, then makes the final decision about which expert witness was most believable:

> This is a state of affairs that doctors, who tend to be authoritarian and who often take themselves and their opinions seriously, find deplorable. Many of the proposals of recent years—that technical matters concerning sanity, medical diagnoses, and other medical matters be removed from the arena of the adversary procedure and put into the hands of a panel or group of experts acting as consultants to the court—have their origin in the wounded vanity of medical experts. Those who push hardest to remove much of the subject of the trial from the trial procedure are often those least aware of the protection to individual liberties that is the product of the adversary system, and the least knowledgeable about the long history of hardfought victories that has culminated in the unwieldly and inefficient system of justice, which in spite of its drawbacks, deserves such praise as that of Lewis: "Civilization has yet to produce a better system of adjudicating the differences between man and man, and man and institutions, than the Anglo-Saxon administration of law" (Robitscher, 1966).

Robitscher (1966), who is both a psychiatrist and an attorney, does question the weight that is proper to give to psychological or psychiatric testimony, and he cites alternatives: "One typical proposal, put forward with vehemence by a psychiatrist, asks for an impartial examination of the accused before trial and 'preferably before arraignment,' when the issue of insanity has not yet been raised. Another part of this same proposal is the avoidance of the use of the resulting impartial medical testimony until after the guilt or innocence is determined. . . ."

In view of his position on the rights of the person to expert testimony, as cited in Chapter Six, Robitscher's (1966) position on the expert review versus adversary issue can be summarized as follows:

> Those who wish to take the determination of sanity or mental capacity out of the adversary procedure arena overlook the fact that the jury system was brought into being to safeguard the rights of the individual, that it acts in criminal cases (since a unanimous decision is

customarily required for conviction) to weight the balance in favor of the defendant, which is in accordance with our view that innocence is presumed, and that the so-called scientific classification in modern psychiatry has almost as many detractors as it has adherents. They over-look the fact that when matters heretofore determined by jury are allowed to be decided by a board or panel of so-called experts, the individual before the bar has lost some portion of his civil rights. To the lawyer, it seems important that civil rights be preserved; to the psychiatrist, who believes that his diagnosis or prognosis should be accepted without challenge, these rights seem less important.

There seems little doubt that the expert review approach would allow for greatest reliability, particularly inter-judge reliability, because accepted criteria on which to base the judgment would probably be adopted by each review group from the onset. This is, however, an excellent issue to use as a case in point regarding reliability, namely that the maintenance of rights, with all of the philosophical and political concomitants, seems to win out over what might seem like the most "professional" (albeit potentially a sterile and unhumanistic) posture.

As has probably been deduced by this point, expert testimony carries differing weight within judicial proceedings. In an effort to refocus to a proper perspective, the weighting ranges from, for all practical purposes, allowing the expert witness to make the judicial decision and, at least in some cases, prescribing the "sentence," to situations where the expert witness is placed in a very impotent, demeaning role. Regarding the latter, Robitscher (1966) provides an interesting quote from one judge who instructed the jury as follows: "You will consider the opinions of the psychiatrists. You must consider their training, qualifications and experience, and the date or dates when they examined the defendant. It must be kept in mind that an opinion is considered of low grade and not entitled to much weight against positive testimony of actual facts such as statements by the defendant and observations of his actions."

It is likely that some professionals, particularly those with faulty professional identities or personal insecurity, would interpret such instructions to a jury as being demeaning. In point of fact, it would seem that this judge's statement is in strong accord with the behavioral scientist's view about how expert testimony should be weighted: *expert testimony is but opinion, it is not fact, and therefore both reliability and validity are undetermined.*

As with the case of a judge's instructions regarding the weighting of expert testimony, the reliability of the expert testimony if also affected by the attitudes reflected toward it by the attorneys. As mentioned earlier, Haggerty, Kane, and Udall (1972) have commented on the naivete of attorneys in relationship to understanding mental retardation and, consequently, in optimally representing persons who are mentally retarded. Roberts (1968) notes that: "Attorneys frequently have little idea of the standard they should require a psychiatrist to fulfill when he testifies. Before discussing standards, however, it is necessary to raise a preliminary point. Psychiatrists may feel, either consciously or unconsciously, that their testimony must be guarded. . . ."

The point here is that the attorney has a critical role to fulfill: he must be capable personally of appreciating the perimeter of the expert witness's competencies and must communicate with him in such a way as to maximize his, the expert witness's, effectiveness. In other words, there must be a mutual understanding of and respect for the roles, functions, capabilities, and responsibilities between the attorney and the expert witness. Otherwise, less than optimal reliability in the testimony will be the outcome.

Another source of potential influence on the reliability of expert testimony is within the lexical realm. Here there are two vantage points. On one hand, the expert witness, e.g. a psychiatrist, is being asked to communicate in legal language, and as with any "foreign traveler," his expertise with the language can lead to ambiguity, e.g. note the discussion in the *Cahill v. Cahill* case (Allen, Ferster, and Rubin, 1968). Conversely, the psychiatrist has the distinct psychiatric language for describing his expert opinions, and yet this language is directed at non-professionals, namely laymen constituting a jury (and, of course, their reaction to psychiatric terminology and/or jargon could also fit into a "foreign traveler" model). Therefore, an essential ingredient for maximizing effectiveness and consequently reliability in expert testimony is to take steps to assure that communication channels are open and, relatedly, that the "language" being used means the same thing to the sender and the receiver e.g. the psychiatrist-professional communicating with the laymen jury members.

Time for involvement is another factor that affects reliability of expert testimony. Bellamy (1968) states: "Judges have weeks in which to study a case and their deliberations are made in the relative calm of private chambers. By contrast, the physician-psychiatrist testifies under oath; his advance study and preparation do not always prepare him for certain questions which (if he can formulate an opinion) he is under a legal duty to answer; and he does this under the heat of cross examination. . . ."

This quote illustrates one way in which the time element enters into affecting reliability of expert testimony: expert opinions must often be formulated quickly, without advanced scholarly study for the question *per se,* and in an atmosphere that is sometimes discrediting or demeaning (such as in the case of a prosecutor cross-examining a defendant's expert witness). Another way in which time enters into the expert testimony is the evaluation of the defendant; that is, the amount of time devoted by an expert witness to some sort of evaluation, such as a psychiatric examination or the administration of psychological tests, has to be paid for by someone, and the mere pragmatic issue of cost sometimes leads to a devoting of less than optimum amount of time to the evaluation. This, of course, could lead to an expert witness speaking with less authority, in the sense that he has limited data and that his statements would (or could) be more authoritative if he were able to devote more time to the evaluation (and to the testimony as well, at least in some cases).

The answer to many of the reliability questions raised herein seems to boil down to an improved state of affairs between the legal profession and the mental health professions, such as between attorneys and the mental health professionals who could serve as expert witnesses. Bazelon (1968) has given strong support to bringing behavioral scientists into the legal processes, and he recognizes that it is a matter, at least in part, of being oriented to the potential contributions from mutual involvement; he also recognizes that this need for orientation extends beyond the practitioners directly involved in case handling: "Nor is it just the judges and lawyers who need education. The whole legislative process requires it."

## EXPERT TESTIMONY FOR RIGHTS

The preceding section has been devoted primarily to expert testimony in situations involving liability, namely criminal proceedings. Also the final paragraph in the last section moves toward the interdisciplinary unity that can culminate in another form of legal benefits for the mentally retarded from expert testimony: the upholding of rights.

It should be promptly clarified that the usage of "upholding rights" is not limited to formal legal proceedings. Indeed, the use of expert testimony in this area would probably be maximal in non-legal contexts, such as administrative situations. Further, the "rights" need not be the most obvious constitutional rights, but might well be the more subtle rights that should accrue with normalization (a principal topic of the next chapter).

In the past, many service delivery systems (such as the public school system) have formulated their own policies, ostensibly designed to be in the best interest of their constituency, i.e. the service recipients. But as the facts of reality would have it, there have been countless actions that have been taken for reasons of expediency (particularly financial) at the expense of at least some persons who rightfully should have had access to the benefit of the system. This was, of course, elaborated upon in Chapter Six dealing with the rights of the mentally retarded, and this section needs only to focus on the need for greater professional commitment to and involvement with the provision of expert testimony in non-legal contexts.

Suffice it to say that "professionalism" itself has a construct of "responsible action" within its conceptual composite. Therefore, any professional, regardless of disciplinary identity, is *ethically obligated* to take responsible actions on behalf of those in need. This might be best exemplified by a professional letting certain community action groups know that his expertise, if introduced into their efforts to attain legitimate and honorable objectives, might enhance their probability of goal-fulfillment. Or through the process of community education (e.g. statements in local newspapers, etc.), it might be manifested by having the citizenry become aware that if they are faced with a problem of gaining access to services or other opportunities to which they, as citizens, are entitled, they can fortify their strivings by involving professionals who could evaluate the idiosyncratic conditions, formulate an expert opinion, and communicate via professional testimony to the proper sources.

## CHAPTER TEN

# NORMALIZATION OF THE MENTALLY RETARDED: A CHALLENGE FOR ACTION

THIS BOOK STARTED with a highly personalized *Dedication* section. This concluding chapter is also to be rather personalized, at least more so than some of the other chapters, since the primary thrust is implementation of new attitudes, regulations and laws, and programs and services for the mentally retarded—none of which can attain fruition without a personal commitment and investment in responsible action.

To review briefly, this book has emphasized the role that reliability plays in the legal processes for the mentally retarded; eight dimensions or areas of concern were discussed. First, there was the issue of accomplishing a meaningful definition of the term "mental retardation," and the conclusion was that existing definitions provide at best "a study in ambiguity." Second, diagnostic practices were found to be highly variable in legal proceedings. Third, an analysis of nosological and classification systems revealed that there may be contradictions and/or overlap, and that the underlying philosophies and rationales may differ (such as one system being more reliant upon intelligence quotients than others, or one system being more medically oriented than others). Fourth, the commonly held hypothesis that there is a positive correlation between mental retardation and criminality was found lacking empirical support. Fifth, consideration was given to the legal factors relevant to the common law, statutory, and constitutional rights of the mentally retarded. Sixth, consideration was given to the liability of the mentally retarded. Seventh, it was recognized that administrative and judicial procedures for the mentally retarded are in no way standardized, and that all too often mentally retarded persons tend to receive less than equitable treatment, as compared to non-retarded persons. The eighth and final dimension was the critical role played by professionals in providing expert testimony for cases involving mentally retarded persons.

Analysis of each of these eight dimensions readily reveals that: *Without exception, each of these processes contains evidence and/or examples that unreliable practices are, in fact, applied to the mentally retarded.* The obvious question is: What should be done to improve the situation?

First, let there be no misunderstanding: Improvement is possible! However, improvement will come about only through responsible commitment and action from lay persons and from professionals in all disciplines that deal with the mentally retarded (as well as those professional disciplines that may have only secondary influence on the services afforded to mentally retarded persons).

Perhaps the most critical single guideline for the much needed responsible commitment and action is: *Normalization.* Normalization, in this context, would mean that professional helping services (such as those offered by educators, mental and physical health specialists, social service workers, and legal practitioners, to name but a few of the sources) should strive to promote, via their "therapeutic" interventions (generically defined) *behavior for the mentally retarded that will be looked upon by others as "normal."*

In the past, mental retardation and other handicapping conditions were given recognition because of *exceptionality.* The pendulum has swung in the other direction. Why? Because various professional indices have demonstrated that emphasis upon deviancy or exceptionality results only in continued deviancy or exceptionality. The therapeutic and/or educational interventions may have brought about behavior that the public deemed "acceptable"—but it was "acceptable" because the person in question was recognized as being deviant. In other words, he had been "branded" eligible for special considerations because of his handicapping condition (s).

The foregoing comment does not mean, in any manner, that persons with handicapping conditions, such as the mentally retarded, do not need special considerations. The fact of the matter is, they do! But these special considerations need not segregate them from the general population nor be used to categorize them into accepted exceptionality, and minimize their potential for a relatively normal existence.

It is only through personal commitment that the present situation can change. *Each individual must develop an orientation toward mental retardation that is accurate and just.* While this is of paramount importance to professionals (such as eliminating the fact cited earlier that few attorneys are adequately versed in the legal aspects and psychological/sociological concomitants of mental retardation), it is crucial that this challenge be extended to and met by the general population. Such an involvement will, by necessity, require time and energy to learn about mental retardation (i.e. cognitively), personal ability to make attitudinal alterations (i.e. intrapersonally), and risk-taking to accomplish changes in programmatic and institutional practices (i.e. interpersonally).

Regarding programs and institutions, it almost goes without saying that improvements on behalf of the mentally retarded will necessitate: (1) acknowledgement (in an accurate manner) of the uniqueness of mental retardation; (2) analysis of the existing service system for purposes of identifying strengths and weaknesses relevant to mentally retarded persons who are under its service aegis; and (3) alterations in criteria, policies, guidelines, requirements, practices, and services (i.e. realignment and reallocation of resources) in such a way as to better facilitate the desired normalization processes for the mentally retarded. Stated differently, the programs and institutions should be geared to fulfilling the objectives needed by mentally retarded persons in quest of normalization. Briefly, Johnson (1958) groups the objectives into the trichotomy of "(1) personal or emotional adjustment, (2) social adjustment, and (3) economic adjustment." More broadly stated, the objective is for *programs to be designed primarily to attain maximum normalized behavior for all persons, including the mentally retarded.*

With reference to the right to treatment, it should be recognized that many available educational and psychotherapeutic procedures have not been used with the mentally retarded. The assumption, which is often erroneous, is that the limited intelligence of the mentally retarded renders the helping technique ineffective. In at least some instances, this is based more on the attitude of the professional toward the mentally retarded person than on scientific facts about the handicapping condition and the technique. For example, Woody and Herr (1967) surveyed psychologists who were known to work with mentally retarded persons and found a distinct reluctance to attempt counseling and psychotherapy with the mentally retarded, yet there is evidence that these procedures can promote insight and accomplish behavioral change for the mentally retarded (see also Woody, 1966). It seems of particular importance to further explore the use of behavioral modification techniques with the mentally retarded, although the behavioral approach should not be seen as a panacea. As may be evidenced by perusal of professional journals, such as the *American Journal of Mental Deficiency* and the *Journal of Applied Behavior Analysis,* there have been many successful applications of behavioral modification systems to mentally retarded persons (including severely retarded persons requiring custodial treatment); several examples are cited by Woody (1969, 1971).

Regardless of the educational or therapeutic technique used, it is of the utmost importance that educators and mental health specialists set aside long standing stereotypes of a particular discipline's functioning, and strive instead for a unification of services; i.e. *there should be professional complementarianism.* Cleavage between the helping professional disciplines is defeating and eventually detrimental to society, the professional disciplines, and, of course, the persons in need of professional help.

Finally, the legal system has the onus of responsibility upon its shoulders to better meet the needs of the mentally retarded. The relevance of mental retardation to particular legal concepts of practices must be clarified. In practical terms, laws must be examined and perhaps changed (or, indeed, perhaps new laws instituted) that will both properly recognize the relevant aspects of mental retardation in the legal proceedings and lead to judicial decisions and administrative action that are compatible with the quest for normalization. The lay person, the attorney, the judge, the educator, the health professional—any single person—can be the initial stimulus for promoting administrative, legal practice, or legislative changes: this would be meeting the challenge to work for responsible commitment and action for the normalization of mentally retarded persons.

Throughout this book and within this final chapter particularly, there is the underlying assumption that successful change will be accomplished by a multi-leveled strategy. The previously discussed "professional complementarianism" is one example. Some strategies may focus on the institutional level, while others focus on the individual level. However, the beginning of change can come about only if the individuals are dedicated to the concept of normalization and begin responsible action: *laymen and professionals of all ilk must meet this challenge in the name of humanitarianism.*

# REFERENCES


Abeson, A. (Ed.): *A Continuing Summary of Pending and Completed Litigation Regarding the Education of Handicapped Children.* Arlington, Va., Council for Exceptional Children, 1973.

Abramson, M. F.: The criminalization of mentally disordered behavior: Possible side-effect of a new mental health law. *Hospital and Community Psychiatry,* 1972, vol. 23, 4 (April), pp. 101-105.

Allen, R. C.: Legal norms and practices affecting the mentally deficient. *American Journal of Orthopsychiatry,* 1968, vol. 38, pp. 635-642.

Allen, R. C., Ferster, Elyce Zenoff, and Rubin, J. G. (Eds.): *Readings in Law and Psychiatry.* Baltimore, Johns Hopkins, 1968.

American Psychiatric Association: *Diagnostic and Statistical Manual of Mental Disorders* (2nd ed.). Washington, D.C., American Psychiatric Association, 1968.

Arbuckle, D. G.: *Counseling: Philosophy, Theory, and Practice.* Boston, Allyn and Bacon, 1965.

Bazelon, D. L.: Mental retardation: Some legal and moral considerations. *American Journal of Orthopsychiatry,* 1968, vol. 35, pp. 838-844.

Bazelon, D. L.: Implementing the right to treatment. *University of Chicago Law Review,* 1969, vol. 36, pp. 742-754.

Bellamy, W. A.: Malpractice in psychiatry. In R. C. Allen, Elyce Z. Ferster, and J. G. Rubin (Eds.): *Readings in Law and Psychiatry.* Baltimore, Johns Hopkins, 1968, pp. 300-304.

Beller, E. K.: *Clinical Process.* New York, Free Press in Glencoe, 1962.

Benton, A. L.: Psychological evaluation and differential diagnosis. In H. A. Stevens and R. Heber (Eds.): *Mental Retardation: A Review of Research.* Chicago, University of Chicago Press, 1964, pp. 16-56.

Bray, J. J.: The legal rights of the mentally retarded in relation to their civil liberties. *Australian Journal of Mental Retardation,* 1971, vol. 1, pp. 133-140.

Brodsky, S. L., and Robey, A.: On becoming an expert witness: Issues of orientation and effectiveness. *Professional Psychology,* 1972, vol. 3, pp. 173-176.

Brown v. Board of Education: *Federal Supplement* (1954), vol. 347, pp. 483-493.

Brown, B. S., Courtless, T. F., and Silber, D.: Fantasy and force: A study of the dynamics of the mentally retarded offender. *Journal of Criminal Law, Criminology, and Police Science,* 1970, vol. 61, pp. 71-77.

Brown, B. S., and Courtless, T. F.: The mentally retarded in penal and correctional institutions. *American Journal of Psychiatry,* 1968, vol. 124 (part 2), pp. 1164-1169.

Browning, R. M.: Effects of irrelevant peripheral visual stimuli on discrimination learning in minimally brain damaged children. *Journal of Consulting Psychology,* 1967, vol. 31, pp. 371-376.

Chambers, D. L., III.: Some comments on the administration of the insanity defense. *Law Quadrangle Notes* (University of Michigan Law School), 1972, vol. 16, pp. 3, 7-13.

Curran, W. J.: Tort liability of the mentally ill and mentally deficient. *Ohio State Law Journal,* 1960, vol. 21, pp. 52-74.

Davidson, H. A.: *Forensic Psychiatry* (2nd ed.). New York, Ronald Press, 1965.

Deutsch, A.: *The Mentally Ill in America.* New York, Columbia University Press, 1946.

Dix, G. E.: Psychological abnormality as a factor in grading criminal liability: Diminished capacity, diminished responsibility, and the like. *Journal of Criminal Law, Criminology, and Police Science,* 1971, vol. 62, pp. 313-334.

Doll, E. A.: The essentials of an inclusive concept of mental deficiency. *American Journal of Mental Deficiency,* 1941, vol. 46, pp. 214-219.

Ennis, B. J., and Friedman, P. R. (Eds.): *Legal Rights of the Mentally Handicapped. Volume One.* New York, Practising Law Institute and the Mental Health Law Project, 1973a.

Ennis, B. J., and Friedman, P. R. (Eds.): *Legal Rights of the Mentally Handicapped. Volume Two.* New York, Practising Law Institute and the Mental Health Law Project, 1973b.

Ennis, B. J., and Friedman, P. R. (Eds.): *Legal Rights of the Mentally Handicapped. Volume Three.* New York, Practising Law Institute and the Mental Health Law Project, 1973c.

Ferster, Elyce Zenoff: Eliminating the unfit—is sterilization the answer? *Ohio State Law Journal,* 1966, vol. 27, pp. 591-633.

Friedman, P.: *Mental Retardation and the Law: A Report on Status of Current Court Cases.* Washington, D.C., Office of Mental Retardation Coordination, 1973.

Gatti, D. J., and Gatti, R. D.: *The Teacher and the Law.* West Nyack, N.Y., Parker, 1972.

Glueck, S.: *Law and Psychiatry: Cold War or Entente Cordiale?* Baltimore, Johns Hopkins Press, 1966.

Gruenberg, E. M.: Epidemiology. In H. A. Stevens and R. Heber (Eds.): *Mental Retardation: A Review of Research.* Chicago, University of Chicago, 1964, pp. 259-306.

Haggerty, D. E., Kane, L. A., Jr., and Udall, D. K.: An essay on the legal rights of the mentally retarded. *Family Law Quarterly,* 1972, vol. 6, pp. 59-71.

Hansen, R. W., and Goldberg, S. J.: Casework in a family court. *Social Casework,* 1967, vol. 48, pp. 416-421.

Harvard Law Review Association: Requiring a criminal defendant to submit to a government psychiatric examination: An invasion of the privilege against self-incriminations. *Harvard Law Review,* 1970, vol. 83, pp. 648-671.

Heber, R.: Modifications in the manual of terminology and classification in mental retardation. *American Journal of Mental Deficiency,* 1961, vol. 65, pp. 499-500.

Helmstadter, G. C.: *Principles of Psychological Measurement.* New York, Appleton-Century-Crofts, 1964.

Hess, J. H., Pearsall, H. B., Slichter, D. A., and Thomas, H. E.: Competency to stand trial. In R. C. Allen, Elyce Z. Ferster, and J. G. Rubin (Eds.) : *Readings in Law and Psychiatry.* Baltimore, Johns Hopkins, 1968, pp. 379-388.

Hinkle, V. R.: Legal rights of the mentally retarded. *American Journal of Mental Deficiency,* 1959, vol. 63, pp. 501-505.

Hinkle, V. R.: Alternatives to test of criminal responsibility. *Crime and Delinquency,* 1964, vol. 10, pp. 110-116.

Hobson v. Hansen: *Federal Supplement* (July 19, 1967) , vol. 269, pp. 401-518.

Hofling, C. K.: Criminal responsibility in the Durham rule: An editorial. *Hospital and Community Psychiatry,* 1972, vol. 23, 4 (April) , pp. 6-7.

Holmes, L. B., Moser, H. W., Halldorsson, S., Mack, Cornelia, Pant, S. S., and Matzilevich, B.: *Mental Retardation: An Atlas of Diseases With Associated Physical Abnormalities.* New York, Macmillan, 1972.

Hutt, L., and Gibby, G.: *The Mentally Retarded Child: Development, Education and Treatment* (2nd ed.) . Boston, Allyn and Bacon, 1965.

Jaslow, R. I., and Smith, S. V.: A proposal for a new conceptual use of the term "mental retardation." *Mental Retardation,* 1972, vol. 10, pp. 36-37.

Johnson, G. O.: The education of mentally handicapped children. In W. M. Cruickshank and G. O. Johnson (Eds.) : *Education of Exceptional Children and Youth.* Englewood Cliffs, N.J., Prentice-Hall, 1958, pp. 189-226.

Kay, Herma H., Farnham, Louise J., Karren, Beth D., Knakal, Jeanne, and Diamond, Priscilla M.: Legal planning for the mentally retarded: The California experience. *California Law Review,* 1972, vol. 60, pp. 438-529.

Kelly, E. L.: *Assessment of Human Characteristics.* Belmont, Brooks/Cole, 1967.

Kleinmuntz, B.: *Personality Measurement: An Introduction.* Homewood, Dorsey, 1967.

Knudson, J.: Mental retardation—who should pay the bill for resident care in public institutions? *Family Law Quarterly,* 1969, vol. 3, pp. 331-343.

Kolasa, B. J.: Psychology and law. *American Psychologist,* 1972, vol. 27, pp. 599-603.

Lehman, Virginia: Guardianship and protective services for older people. *Social Casework,* 1961, vol. 42, pp. 252-257.

Levy, R. J.: Protecting the mentally retarded: An empirical survey and evaluation of state guardianship in Minnesota. *Minnesota Law Review,* 1965, vol. 49, pp. 821-887.

Levy, S.: The role of mental deficiency in the causation of criminal behavior. *American Journal of Mental Deficiency,* 1953, vol. 58, pp. 455-463.

Lippman, L., and Goldberg, I. I.: *Right to Education: Anatomy of the Pennsylvania Case and Its Implications for Exceptional Children.* New York, Teachers College Press, 1973.

Livermore, J. M., Malmquist, C. P., and Meehl, P. E.: Justification for civil commitment. *University of Pennsylvania Law Review,* 1968, vol. 117, pp. 75-96.

Livermore, J. M., and Meehl, P. E.: The virtues of M'Naghten. *Minnesota Law Review,* 1967, vol. 51, pp. 789-856.

Masland, R. L., Sarason, S. B., and Gladwin, T.: *Mental Subnormality: Biological, Psychological, and Cultural Factors.* New York, Basic Books, 1958.

McAllister, E. W. C.: Thoughts on the use of the term mental retardation. *Mental Retardation,* 1972, vol. 10, 6 (Dec.), pp. 40-41.

Mental Health Law Project: *Basic Rights of the Mentally Handicapped.* Washington, D.C., Mental Health Law Project, 1973.

Mills, *et al.* v. District of Columbia Board of Education. *Federal Supplement* (August 1, 1972), vol. 348, pp. 866-883.

Mitchell, B. C.: A glossary of measurement terms. *Test Service Notebook 13.* New York, Harcourt Brace Jovanovich, undated.

Mitchell, K. M., and Namenek, T. M.: A comparison of therapist and client social class. *Professional Psychology,* 1970, vol. 1, pp. 225-230.

Morris, G. H. (Ed.): *The Mentally Ill and the Right to Treatment.* Springfield, Thomas, 1970.

Murdock, C. W.: Civil rights of the mentally retarded: Some critical issues. *Notre Dame Lawyer,* 1972, vol. 48, pp. 133-188.

Ober, Grace G.: Some aspects on legal guardianship for the adult mentally retarded. *American Journal of Mental Deficiency,* 1963, vol. 68, pp. 15-23.

Ogg, Elizabeth: *Securing the Legal Rights of Retarded Persons.* Public Affairs Pamphlet No. 492. New York, Public Affairs Committee, 1973.

Pacht, A. R., Kuehn, Jayne K., Bassett, H. T., and Nash, M. M.: The current status of the psychologist as an expert witness. *Professional Psychology,* 1973, vol. 4, pp. 409-413.

Pasamanick, B., Dinitz, S., and Lefton, M.: Psychiatric orientation and its relation to diagnosis and treatment in a mental hospital. *American Journal of Psychiatry,* 1959, vol. 116, pp. 127-132.

Pennsylvania Association of Retarded Children v. The Commonwealth of Pennsylvania: *Federal Supplement* (October 8, 1971), vol. 334, pp. 1257-1269.

Polier, Justine Wise: *The Rule of Law and the Role of Psychiatry.* Baltimore, Johns Hopkins, 1968.

President's Committee on Mental Retardation (Legal Rights Work Group): *Compendium of Class Action Law Suits Related to the Legal Rights of the Mentally Retarded.* Washington, D.C., President's Committee on Mental Retardation (April 24), 1973.

Pyfer, J. F., Jr.: The juvenile's right to receive treatment. *Family Law Quarterly,* 1972, vol. 6, pp. 279-320.

Redmount, R. S.: The use of psychologists in legal practice. In B. Lubin and E. E. Levitt (Eds.): *The Clinical Psychologist: Background, Roles, and Functions.* Chicago, Aldine, 1967, pp. 267-275.

Roberts, L. M.: Some observations on the problems of the forensic psychiatrist. In R. C. Allen, Elyce Z. Ferster, and J. G. Rubin (Eds.): *Readings in Law and Psychiatry.* Baltimore, Johns Hopkins, 1968, pp. 136-145.

Robitscher, J. D.: *Pursuit of Agreement: Psychiatry and the Law.* Philadelphia, Lippincott, 1966.

Robitscher, J.: Medical limits of criminality. *Annals of Internal Medicine,* 1970, vol. 73, pp. 849-851.

Robitscher, J.: Courts, state hospitals, and the right to treatment. *American Journal of Psychiatry,* 1972a, vol. 129, pp. 298-304.

Robitscher, J.: The changing face of legal psychiatry: Or social legal psychiatry. Unpublished paper delivered at the Annual Meeting of the American College of Legal Medicine in Miami, May 13, 1972b.

Robinson, H. B., and Robinson, Nancy M.: *The Mentally Retarded Child: A Psychological Approach.* New York, McGraw-Hill, 1965.

Rollin, H. R.: *The Mentally Abnormal Offender and the Law.* New York, Pergamon, 1969.

Rowden, D. W., Michel, J. B., Dillehay, R. C. and Martin, H. W.: Judgments about candidates for psychotherapy: The influence of social class and insight-verbal ability. *Journal of Health and Social Behavior,* 1970, vol. 11, pp. 51-58.

Sarason, B.: *Psychological Problems in Mental Deficiency* (3rd ed.). New York, Harper, 1959.

Schwartz, W. D., Jr., and Dumpman, Shirley: Voluntary commitment by persuasion. *Hospital and Community Psychiatry,* 1972, vol. 23, 4 (April), pp. 128-129.

Shong, Ellenmarie: The legal responsibility of parents for their children's delinquency. *Family Law Quarterly,* 1972, vol. 6, pp. 145-178.

Smith, J. O.: Criminality and mental retardation. *Training School Bulletin,* 1962, vol. 59, 3 (Nov.), pp. 74-80.

Stevens, H. A.: Overview. In H. A. Stevens and R. Heber (Eds.): *Mental Retardation: A Review of Research.* Chicago, University of Chicago, 1964, pp. 1-15.

Strodtbeck, F. L., Simon, Rita J., and Hawkins, C.: Social status and jury deliberations. In R. I. Evans and R. M. Rozelle (Eds.) : *Social Psychology in Life*. Boston, Allyn and Bacon, 1970, pp. 269-282.

Suarez, J. M.: Psychiatry and the criminal law system. *American Journal of Psychiatry,* 1972, vol. 129, pp. 293-297.

Szasz, T. S.: *Law, Liberty, and Psychiatry*. New York, Collier Books, 1968.

Szasz, T. S. and Alexander, G. J.: Law, property, and psychiatry. *American Journal of Orthopsychiatry,* 1972, vol. 42, pp. 610-626.

Temerlin, M. K.: Diagnostic bias in community mental health. *Community Mental Health Journal,* 1970, vol. 6, pp. 110-117.

Thorne, F. C.: Clinical judgment: A study of clinical error. Brandon, Vt., *Journal of Clinical Psychology,* 1961.

Tredgold, A. F.: *A Text-book of Mental Deficiency* (6th ed.) . Baltimore, William Wood, 1937.

United Nations: United Nations' declaration on the rights of mentally retarded persons, December 20, 1971.

Wechsler, D.: *Manual: Wechsler Adult Intelligence Scale*. New York, Psychological Corp., 1955.

Woody, R. H.: Counseling the mentally subnormal: An American model. *Journal of Mental Subnormality,* 1966, vol. 12, pp. 37-39.

Woody, R. H.: *Behavioral Problem Children in the Schools: Recognition, Diagnosis, and Behavioral Modification.* New York, Appleton-Century-Crofts, 1969.

Woody, R. H.: *Psychobehavioral Counseling and Therapy: Integrating Behavioral and Insight Techniques.* New York, Appleton-Century-Crofts, 1971.

Woody, R. H.: The counselor-therapist and clinical assessment. In R. H. Woody and Jane D. Woody (Eds.) : *Clinical Assessment in Counseling and Psychotherapy*. New York, Appleton-Century-Crofts, 1972, pp. 1-29.

Woody, R. H., and Billy, Heidi T.: Influencing the intelligence scores of retarded and nonretarded boys with clinical suggestion. *American Journal of Clinical Hypnosis,* 1970, vol. 12, pp. 268-271.

Woody, R. H., and Herr, E. L.: Mental retardation and clinical hypnosis. *Mental Retardation,* 1967, vol. 5, pp. 27-38.

Woody, R. H., and Woody, Jane D. (Eds.) : *Clinical Assessment in Counseling and Psychotherapy*. New York, Appleton-Century-Crofts, 1972.

Wyatt v. Stickney: *Federal Supplement* (March 12, 1971) , vol. 325, pp. 781-786.

Wyatt v. Stickney: *Federal Supplement* (December 10, 1971) , vol. 334, pp. 1341-1344.

# NAME INDEX

# SUBJECT INDEX

## D

## N

## S